C0-AWP-235

GOD'S SECRET

F · O · R

GETTING THINGS DONE

BRUCE COOK

While this book is designed for the reader's personal enjoyment and profit, it is also intended for group study. A Leader's Guide with Victor Multiuse Transparency Masters is available from your local bookstore or from the publisher.

VICTOR

BOOKS a division of SP Publications, Inc.

WHEATON, ILLINOIS 60187

Offices also in
Whitby, Ontario, Canada
Amersham-on-the-Hill, Bucks, England

Most of the Scripture quotations in this book are from the *New American Standard Bible* (NASB), © the Lockman Foundation 1960, 1962, 1963, 1968, 1971, 1972, 1973, 1975, 1977. Other quotations are from the *King James Version* (KJV); *The Living Bible* (TLB), © 1971, Tyndale House Publishers, Wheaton, IL 60189. Used by permission; and *Holy Bible, New International Version* (NIV), © 1973, 1978, 1984, International Bible Society. Used by permission of Zondervan Bible Publishers.

Recommended Dewey Decimal Classification: 248.1
Suggested Subject Heading: CHRISTIAN LIFE

Library of Congress Catalog Card Number: 83-060819
ISBN: 0-89693-173-0

ABOUT THE AUTHOR

Bruce Cook is founder and president of Leadership Dynamics International. LDI offers biblically based training programs to churches, companies, and Christian organizations. Courses include: Personal Leadership Development, Team Building, Church Faith Planning, Priority Management, Decision Making, Motivation, Marital Team Building, Financial Faith Planning, and Student Leadership Dynamics.

For more information contact:

Leadership Dynamics International
6666 Powers Ferry Road
Suite 120
Atlanta, GA 30339

Contents

ACKNOWLEDGMENTS

I would like to express sincere appreciation to Bill Bright, whose commitment to a life of faith helped spark the idea of faith planning; Cathy Hustedt, whose editing skills contributed greatly to the initial formulation of the book; Jim Heiskell, for his ideas, feedback, insight, and encouragement during the final stages of writing; and my secretary, Diane Trawicky, for her tireless efforts in the typing and retyping of the manuscript.

To my loving wife Donna,
whose constant encouragement
made this book possible.

Introduction

As a new Christian, I remember vividly the evenings I spent exploring God's Word. I was overjoyed at discovering that God not only wanted me to spend eternity with Him in heaven, but that He had a plan for me on earth. This plan called for me to allow Christ to be Lord of my life. I, Bruce Cook, could draw on the unlimited resources of God to meet all of my needs.

This discovery came none too soon, for shortly thereafter my world fell apart. The girl to whom I was engaged couldn't understand what had happened to me. After several agonizing weeks of trying to share my discovery with her, she broke the engagement. I was shattered! The following week my father died.

It was during this dark time that the Lord demonstrated His faithfulness to me. As I turned to Him, I experienced His peace. Though my circumstances were sad, His joy filled my heart. The Lord met every need I had. It was no longer I, but Christ who lived in me! I was learning the reality of the words, "My God shall supply all your needs according to His riches" (Phil. 4:19). As the weeks went by, I met several other Christians on campus and became involved in a church nearby. Every time the door was open I was there and, as a result, I became involved in the inner workings of a church.

I will never forget my first planning meeting. The committee was discussing the need to build a new educational building. One of the church leaders admitted that it was a need, but he said the church didn't have the resources. I recall that my immediate thought was, "What about *God's* resources? If He can meet my personal needs, can't He also meet His church's needs?" Since I was a new member of the church and didn't want to sound too "spiritual," I kept quiet. "Maybe the problem of planning without trusting God to meet our needs is just in this church," I thought.

Unfortunately, during 14 years of consulting with scores of Christian organizations, churches, and Christian executives, I have seen that planning without faith is the norm! Several weeks ago I was in a meeting to discuss how a group of downtown churches can better meet the increasing challenge of feeding and housing an estimated 2,000 homeless people in our city. As we were discussing how to tap the resources of God's church in our community to meet the need, one pastor quickly spoke up: "You don't really think we can solve the problem, do you?" He didn't realize it, but he had put his finger on the problem. He was looking only at his limited resources. He was not taking into account God's unlimited resources!

We often approach personal, church, family, or organizational planning as if it were based totally on our resources and not God's. We have not appropriated the lordship of Jesus Christ to our plans. As a result, we are limiting what God wants to accomplish in our society today.

The process of faith planning has evolved out of this need

to provide a practical way to build faith into our plans—to tap God's resources and to enlighten our minds to what God wants to accomplish through us.

The faith-planning process works. It was used during the "Here's Life, America" campaign to mobilize over 12,000 churches and 350,000 laypersons in 18 months. It has been used on an individual basis by thousands of Christian business and professional people who have attended our Leadership Dynamics seminars, and by scores of churches to help their memberships develop a greater vision and conviction of what God wants to do through their local fellowships. In all walks of life, Christians are stepping out boldly in new dimensions of trust and faith.

Whatever our areas of responsibility, we need to build faith into our plans—not only to please God ("without faith it is impossible to please Him" [Heb. 11:6]), but to experience the joy that comes from God's personal involvement in meeting our needs.

We live in a period of great uncertainty and rapid change. The last three decades have lulled many into assuming that the future would simply be a continuation of what has happened in the past, but we are seeing now that this is not the case. Economic uncertainty permeates every level of our society. It affects the household budget, the church budget, the corporate budget, and the national budget. Political uncertainties are commonplace in all parts of the world. There are no longer safe spots of calm and stability. Nations are in turmoil.

How do we plan for the future with so much uncertainty? We plan by faith! Faith "is the assurance of things hoped for, the conviction of things not seen" (Heb. 11:1). Faith is believing the promise of God to meet our needs and to fulfill His desires.

I invite you to join with literally thousands of others who have applied the faith-planning process in their lives, to see

God do the impossible. This book will outline the step-by-step process of planning by faith. At the end of each chapter is a *Personal Application* section. Take the time to apply the principles in each chapter. You will then be putting the faith-planning principles to work immediately in your life. May God richly bless you as you learn to trust Him more.

1
Why Good Plans Fail

In almost any undertaking, there are two surefire ways to fail. One is *not to plan,* and the other is *to plan improperly.* We are admonished to "make plans—counting on God to direct us" (Prov. 16:9, TLB). Without proper planning, it is nearly impossible to become good stewards of the talents and gifts God has given us, to attain our full potential, or to enjoy a measure of success in our lives.

A story of two cub scouts on an overnight camping expedition illustrates the need for proper planning. The boys felt that things were moving too slowly, so they decided to cook a frog. They headed for the nearest stream, carefully lit a fire, and began to boil water in a saucepan from their knapsack. When they spotted a chubby frog relaxing nearby, they quickly tossed the hapless creature into the pot. Just as quickly, he jumped out. They threw him back in. Again, he jumped out of the pot to safety. At this point, the challenge of the boys' adventure had increased considerably, but being enterprising scouts, they eventually came up with an idea that worked. They emptied the hot water from the saucepan, replaced it with cool water from the creek, and set the pan aside. Next, they recaptured the little frog, who had developed a nervous twitch, and flipped him once more into the pot. This time he sat there calmly. In fact a little smile broke out on his face. They placed the saucepan over the flame and, as the water heated slowly, beads of sweat began popping out on the frog's brow. Still he sat there contentedly. As the water gradually became hotter and hotter, the little frog was cooked. He met his demise because he never reached a point where he realized the water was hot enough to cook him.

Nobody actually sets out to lead a mediocre life, but unless we establish goals and develop plans to reach those goals, we may well find ourselves slipping, little by little, into a mediocre existence that deals the deathblow to any sense of accomplishment or fulfillment we might otherwise enjoy.

What is a mediocre existence? Perhaps it can be best described as a life whose focus is on activities that are not inherently bad, but which accomplish little of significance. A typical mediocre life might be spent this way: sleeping, 20 years; watching television, 6 years; waiting for other people, 3 years; and talking on the telephone, 1 year. Without planning, without goal setting, such an existence is likely to develop.

Planning without God

To plan improperly is to plan without looking to God for direction. Non-Christians generally approach plan-making from the standpoint of doing their own thing their own way; they do not actively seek God in the planning process. It is entirely possible for Christians to exclude God from planning if we fail to arrive at those plans through the process of faith. Since we know that without faith it is impossible to please God, we plan to fail when we plan without faith. From God's point of view, our failure is assured.

Two very different planning techniques that are prevalent today may appear harmless, but they can be major stumbling blocks for the Christian. The first, *projection planning,* is taught in most planning or management courses and in many colleges and universities. Its use is widespread among believers and nonbelievers alike. The second technique, which I call *wishful planning,* is more common in the Christian community. It is based on an everyday variety of wishful thinking.

Projection planning is characterized by a focus on the past and a reliance on present resources. For example, projection planners will look at what was accomplished last year and what the trend was in the previous years, then consider the resources they have—such as money or people—and set a goal reflecting an increase based on what has happened in the past.

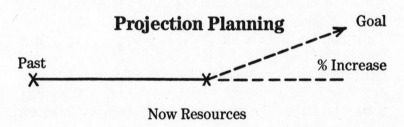

Projection Planning

I recall participating in a planning meeting at a local church in our area. The time had come for each department in the church to present its plans and goals for the coming year. As each person presented his goals, I noticed an amazing trend: Each had simply taken the previous year's attendance, increased it by 10 percent, and made this the goal for the coming year. Then when the pastor finished his presentation of goals for the coming year, he said, "This is what we're trusting God to accomplish through our congregation." In essence, God had become a 10 percent God! Projection-planning goals always seem reasonable enough, as in the case of this church, but the problem occurs in the *process* people go through in setting their goals. They leave faith out of the planning and, therefore, are unable to please God.

A dangerous assumption in projection planning is that conditions will remain the same the coming year; therefore, all we need to do is plan some increase over the previous year. Many businesses are seeing that this principle doesn't work in the economic turbulence of the '80s—that next year simply will not be a repeat of previous years with an increase. In Isaiah we read, "Do not call to mind the former things, or ponder things of the past. Behold, I will do something new" (43:18–19). How can God do something *new* if we're only projecting into the future what has happened in the past with a little something added on? The answer is: He can't!

Another problem for the Christian is that projection planning fails to take into account the resources of the God who owns the cattle on a thousand hills (Ps. 50:10) and "who is able to do immeasurably more than we ask or imagine" (Eph. 3:20, NIV). We, as Christians, do not have to be bound by our own resources, whatever they might be.

Long ago the disciples also overlooked abundant resources that were available to them through Jesus Christ. When Jesus asked them to feed the crowds who had gathered to hear Him, they looked at the five loaves of bread and two fishes that were available and suggested that the people be sent into neighboring villages to buy their own lunches (Mark 6:36). Later the disciples were astonished to see Jesus take the bread and fishes and multiply them to feed the crowd and have some left over. God wants to show us how His unlimited resources are available to meet our needs.

Wishful Planning

Another type of planning that can be a stumbling block for Christians is what I call wishful planning. It evolves something like this: You're sitting in a meeting. An especially persuasive speaker presents a challenge—perhaps to have an evangelistic crusade in your hometown. You become extremely excited, believing that God would like to see such an event take place. So you and your friends draw up plans for the crusade, work hard to make it a success, and then on the evening of the big kickoff rally no one shows up. You and your friends have no idea what went wrong.

My conception of what went wrong is that the people involved set out on what was essentially a faith venture—with no faith at all. We read in Hebrews that faith involved "the *conviction* of things not seen" (11:1). Neither you nor your friends had experienced a deep-seated conviction that God wanted you to launch a crusade in your city; you simply responded emotionally to a heady challenge.

Real life examples of wishful planning are not hard to come by. The other day I read in the paper an account of a very sincere minister whose worthwhile mission ended in bankruptcy even though he claimed to be trusting God. My guess is that his faith was not of the Hebrews 11:1 variety, but was wishful thinking, pure and simple.

Now that we know the dangers, how can we as Christians sidestep the pitfalls of *projection planning*—an approach to planning which limits God from performing the miraculous in our lives, and *wishful planning*—an emotional response in which we step out impulsively, hoping that God will somehow help us accomplish our plans?

Making Plans with God

The remainder of this book will answer that question as we explore the principles of *planning by faith*. This is a scriptural

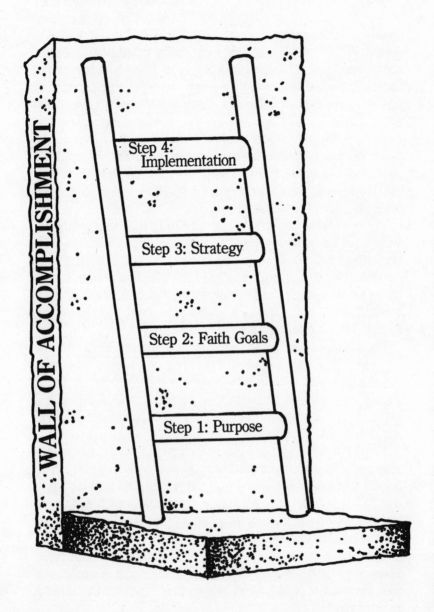

WALL OF ACCOMPLISHMENT

Step 4: Implementation

Step 3: Strategy

Step 2: Faith Goals

Step 1: Purpose

approach that brings together planning technique and faith in such a way that God is both pleased and glorified (because we act every step of the way in faith); our goals are reached (because God intervenes supernaturally in our plans, ensuring their success); and we experience personal growth (because we persevere through difficulties our character is strengthened).

The faith-planning process involves four distinct steps which lead up the ladder of success. Step one calls for understanding our purpose in life. Purpose answers the question *why* and provides a foundation from which to build. Why are we on Planet Earth? Why are we in the particular vocation to which God has called us? Do we clearly understand our mission in life?

Step two involves establishing faith goals. Goals answer the *what.* What specifically do we want to accomplish? Goals provide a sense of direction and focus. They give us something concrete to hang on to when unforeseen circumstances and problems threaten our commitment. Of course, we must be sure we set goals in accord with God's will.

Step three is developing a strategy to meet our goals. We will discover that the key to reaching our goals will come from developing the right strategy. Strategy answers the question *how.* How do we reach the goals we've established? What elements must be built into our plans before we can be successful in accomplishing our goals?

Step four in the faith-planning process is implementing the strategy. It answers *when* and *if.* In this step we will translate our strategies into specific steps and schedules that will take us from where we are to where we want to go. Since not even the best of plans proceed exactly as we schedule them on paper, we must be prepared in this step to make midcourse corrections in strategies when they malfunction. Many of our goals will not be reached unless we learn to alter our course as needed.

PERSONAL APPLICATION

To avoid mediocre life syndrome, let's take the first step up the ladder of success and accomplishment by understanding our life purpose. Begin by thinking about the *Personal Application* questions on the next page and then write your answers.

Goal-Projection Activity
Worksheet

What are some characteristics of a mediocre life?

_____

_____

_____

_____

Identify a projection goal that you've set.

_____

_____

How can you turn your projection goal into a goal that is not tied to what has happened in the past?

_____

_____

_____

_____

2
Understanding Our Mission in Life

Several years ago, on a business trip to the Middle East, I went to Lahore, Pakistan—not the end of the world, perhaps, but you can *see* it from there! As I was heading downtown by car from the airport, I found myself thinking about Atlanta, my hometown. Not long after that, I traveled to Majorca, an island off the coast of Spain. Again, as I was making my trip from the airport to the hotel, I began thinking about Atlanta. Now I am not particularly prone to homesickness, but I can't go anywhere in the world today without thinking of my hometown. Why? Because I see that city's famous product, Coca-Cola, on billboards everywhere I go.

Several years ago it was my privilege to work in the planning office of the Coca-Cola Bottling Company. As part of the orientation program, we were exposed to the fascinating history of Coke. At the turn of the century a pharmacist developed a medicinal product, a syrup. He told his friends, "If your hair is falling out, if your back aches, or if your feet itch, take this syrup; it will cure you." People would buy the syrup and drink it, only to discover that their hair continued to fall out, their backs still ached, and their feet still itched. It was no help as a medicine.

A group of businessmen heard about the product, put some carbonated water in it, and marketed it in a completely different way. They said, "Let's not tell people it will do something for them; let's just say, 'It's the pause that refreshes.' Let's tell people, 'It's the real thing.' Then let's tell them, 'Things go better with Coke.'" In 50 years this company has totally encircled Planet Earth. You can't go anywhere today without finding Coke. How was it done? Those businessmen had a mission that was global in scope. They allocated resources and seriously set out to accomplish their global plan.

God Has a Plan

God too has a plan for Planet Earth, and how much more significant is His plan than that of any business firm. In Isaiah several verses underscore the reality of God's plan: "I will give thanks to Thy name; for Thou hast worked wonders, *plans formed long ago* with perfect faithfulness" (25:1, KJV; italics here and in other Scripture references added by author), and "My purpose will be established, . . . *I have planned it;* surely I will do it" (46:10–11, KJV). These verses and others in Scripture indicate that God does not approach history on a random basis. God speaks with authority and assures us that He will do what He has planned.

In the planning office at the Coca Cola Bottling Company, we literally papered the walls of our offices with charts showing dates when we would accomplish the various steps that would lead to getting a Coke bottle in the hands of everybody on Planet Earth.

I've often thought that if we visited heaven today, perhaps we would see that God has a planning office and on the celestial walls would be charts showing what He wants to accomplish on earth. If God's plans were totally complete, we wouldn't be here—we would be in heaven. In the meantime, His plan for completion includes your city, your community, your company, your church, your family, and you.

Carrying Out God's Plan

Several years ago, Billy Graham wrote his best-selling book *Angels* (Doubleday). In his book he tells of the number of angels at God's beck and call, the power of angels, and their total commitment to obey God's commands. I would have thought that if God wanted to accomplish something on earth, He would utilize this tremendously great resource, angels. But Scripture tells us that God's basic method for accomplishing His plans on earth is through believers—you and me. Scripture indicates that as God wants to accomplish something in a specific neighborhood, community, or country, He raises up individuals through whom He can work to accomplish His plans. We see examples of this in both the Old and New Testaments.

In Exodus we learn that God heard the cry of His people and in His time He moved the Children of Israel out of their bondage in Egypt into the Promised Land. How did God accomplish this significant event? God said to Moses: "Therefore, come now, and I will send you to Pharaoh, so that you may bring My people, the sons of Israel, out of Egypt" (Ex. 3:10). God wanted to move His people out of Egypt so He picked a human instrument by the name of Moses to carry out His plan.

In the New Testament we read, "Set apart for Me Barnabas and Saul for the work to which I have called them" (Acts 13:2). What was that work? In God's timing and economy He wanted to establish churches throughout the Roman Empire. To do that He worked through Saul and Barnabas.

Doing Our Part

God's Word tells us that our purpose in life is to glorify Him. "Every one who is called by My name, and whom I have created for My glory" are the words of the Lord (Isa. 43:7). A key way to glorify God is seen in the life of Christ. At the end of His earthly ministry, Jesus prayed to His heavenly Father, "I glorified Thee on the earth, having accomplished the work which Thou hast given Me to do" (John 17:4, KJV). We glorify God by doing our part of God's plan. What specific work was Jesus given to do? From birth to age 12 we'd have to say he was growing as any child. From ages 12 to 30 Jesus occupied His time as a carpenter, using His hands, becoming a skilled craftsman. From ages 30 to 33 Jesus was an itinerant teacher, and at age 33, He died on the cross. Which of the work was more spiritual? Which brought more glory to His Father in heaven? Jesus glorified His Father in heaven by accomplishing *all* the work He had been given to do. While we may think certain kinds of work are more spiritual than others, we see from the life of Christ that that's not true.

Are we doing the work God has called us to do? Are we following His plan for us? If we are fulfilling that work, not only are we accomplishing something of significance, but we are glorifying our Father in heaven. This becomes exciting!

As we discover how to fulfill our purposes in life, we develop a sense of unity of purpose in all that we do. Without this we are inclined to live compartmentalized lives—to view our business and professional work in one area and our so-called Christian activities in another area.

Though not all of us are asked to deliver God's people from an evil nation or to establish His church throughout an empire, we are *all* called to two distinct types of work: that which is unique to us as individuals, and that which is universal to all believers.

Unique and Universal Work

Unique work has to do with our specific vocation or calling, and is highly personalized. This might involve laboring as a business executive, a homemaker, a pastor, a craftsman, a doctor—whatever best suits our God-given talents and interests. It takes place in the work arena—an office, a home, a school, a store, or whatever location is most appropriate. *Universal work* is to be shared equally by all believers and involves the universal mandates from God concerning such areas as growing to maturity in Christ (Phil. 2:12), discipling others (Matt. 28:19-20), loving one another (John 15:17), building up the body of Christ (Eph. 4:16), meeting the needs of others (Matt. 25), to name but some of the continuing work of believers here on earth.

Our universal work is not innately more spiritual than our unique work, and is not necessarily carried on in places that we might think of as religious, such as a church or a mission field. Our universal work takes place right in the midst of any work arena, within the context of our unique work.

Here is an example: I have a friend in the stock brokerage business who goes to the office (his particular work arena) each day with a twofold goal: to be the best stock broker he can be (his unique work) and to minister to others in the firm (his universal work). Once a week, he holds a Bible study for those of his colleagues whom he has led to Christ. My friend is doing a good job for his company and is using that company as an arena in which to disciple others—a perfect blending of his unique and his universal callings.

We see that as we go about the work (both unique and universal) to which we have been called, we glorify God in the process, and in so doing we fulfill our purpose for being on earth (Isa. 43:7). We find our niche in God's plan.

A Successful Failure

Several years ago, I was responsible for coordinating the distribution of a one-hour evangelistic TV special starring Carol Lawrence and Dean Jones on prime time television in each of the 200 major TV markets.

My colleagues and I had no trouble selling the program to many of the independently owned and operated stations across the country, but in the major television markets of New York, Chicago, Los Angeles, San Francisco, and Philadelphia, the stations owned and operated by the networks refused to sell us prime time for religious programming.

When we heard that the chief executive of one of the major networks was a dedicated Christian, we were delighted, and we quickly made an appointment to meet with him in New York. After a time of warm fellowship, we played a video cassette recording of our show. After a few minutes, the executive turned off the recorder and announced, "That program will never get on the air as long as I am president of this network!"

He went on to admit that there was nothing wrong with the quality of the film—in fact, it was among the best films he had seen in a long time. Though he was in a position to make exceptions to the company policy, he did not feel that his Christianity should affect his professional and business decisions, he said. It would not be a good "business" decision.

Six weeks later, this high-ranking executive was suddenly fired for no apparent reason by the chairman of the board. I personally feel that God may have been testing His servant, and he came up short. The man's focus was so firmly fixed on his climb up the corporate ladder (his unique work) that he lost sight of the universal work which he was called to do. His lot was not unlike that of the Pharisees and lawyers who "rejected God's purpose for themselves" (Luke 7:30) and therefore were not used by God.

Success Is Doing God's Work

Success for the Christian can be defined as *determining what God wants to accomplish and then getting in on it.* The network executive had a clear-cut opportunity to get in on the action by spreading the Word of God in an effective manner, and he blew it. No one will ever know what would have happened had he taken a chance and aired the program in question.

In the sixth century B.C., there were several thousand Jews living in exile in Babylonia. All of them had turned from the ways of the Lord. They were deeply immersed in idolatry and the vilest forms of immorality. Commenting on this situation, God said to His Prophet Ezekiel, "I searched for a man among them who should build up the wall and stand in the gap before Me for the land, that I should not destroy it; but I found no one" (Ezek. 22:30). Not one was willing to respond to the call of his universal work on this earth, and God did, in fact, destroy the land as He said He would.

Today, I believe there are "lands" that God wants to save. Those "lands" may be in our companies, our communities, or wherever God has placed us to be available instruments. We must recognize our higher calling (to glorify God) and be available to be used by God to accomplish His plan in our sphere of influence.

(Personal Application, next page)

PERSONAL APPLICATION

Write in your own words what you believe your purpose in life is. My purpose in life is to _____

_____

_____

What is the *unique* work to which God has called you?

_____

_____

From Scripture make a list of the *universal* work that God has called you to do in the context of your *unique* work.

_____

_____

_____

_____

_____

_____

3
Forming a Faith Partnership with God

In determining an approach and attitude toward our work, we can look at Jesus as our example. "My food is to do the will of Him who sent Me, and to accomplish His work" (John 4:34). Jesus considered His work on earth as important to His life as the food that sustained Him physically. He did not, as we are inclined to do, think up various projects on His own and then forge ahead with His plans. In fact, He did nothing on His own initiative, seeking instead the will of the Father in all things (John 5:30). Jesus determined what it was that God wanted Him to do, and then He got on with the prescribed business. His was a perfect working relationship with the Father: the One initiating, the Other following through. In John we read Jesus' answer to the Jews: "My Father is working until now, and I Myself am working" (John 5:17). Jesus and the Father worked together.

This is the way we are to function in relation to Christ. Jesus said, "I am the vine, you are the branches; he who abides in Me, and I in him, he bears much fruit; for apart from Me you can do nothing" (John 15:5). Jesus' role is to initiate and empower; we are to bear the fruit. Such an arrangement constitutes a unique partnership between God and man.

The Nature of a Partnership

Several years ago, I helped put together a partnership comprised of 10 individuals whose aim it was to produce and market a Christian film. My job was to do the actual producing and marketing; the others involved were to put up the necessary funds. Our tasks were not equal, but as each of us fulfilled his part of the bargain, the project was completed. Such is the nature of a partnership.

In a partnership between God and man, the partners certainly are not equal in terms of power and authority, but as God and man work together, each fulfilling his specific function, a predetermined goal is met. In fact, what may have been deemed impossible from the human viewpoint is often accomplished as a matter of course. Such is the result of allowing God to work through us.

When we enter into a partnership with God, the division of labor will always follow the same format. Let's focus first on God's role in the partnership. Three ways God is involved will greatly influence how we should plan:

First, God has promised to *direct* us. "I will instruct you and teach you in the way in which you should go; I will counsel you with My eye on you" (Ps. 32:8). In another Psalm we have God's promise to direct the way of those who fear Him. "Who is the man who fears the Lord? He will instruct him in the way he should choose" (25:12).

Second, God has promised to *meet our needs.* "They who seek the Lord shall not be in want of any good thing" (Ps. 34:10). God has promised to "supply all your needs according to His riches in glory in Christ Jesus" (Phil. 4:19).

Third, God has promised to *reward* us, for "He is a rewarder of those who seek Him" (Heb. 11:6). This last promise is not as much emphasized in our Christian teaching today, but it is certainly as valid as any of the other promises of God.

Amazing as it may seem, the God of the universe has actually promised to direct our steps in all that we do, to provide us with whatever we need to accomplish our goals, and then to reward our efforts. Such an arrangement is almost too wonderful to contemplate, but it is only half of the bargain. We must fulfill our functions as well.

Our Role

The Bible tells us that our responsibility is to have faith and to act in accordance with that faith. Just as we once entered into a relationship with God by means of faith (Eph. 2:8–9), so are we to continue to live by faith (Rom. 1:12) at every moment of our lives, for it is faith that serves as the catalyst to release God's tremendous power to work in us and through us. Jesus could do no mighty works in Nazareth because of their unbelief (lack of faith).

To say that our part is simply to have faith may at first sound trite and oversimplified, but a careful examination of genuine faith as the Bible describes it reveals that this is not the case. A child once described the phenomenon of faith as "believing a thing is true, even when you know it's not." We laugh, but I'm sure we all can identify with that statement because we have been guilty of exercising that kind of "faith."

For some Christians, faith entails basic unbelief in a scriptural precept or promise coupled with a tiny hope that *maybe* it is true. When we want a promise to be fulfilled, we try desperately to muster the faith (which we regard as a feeling) to enable God to act, and then we try to somehow sustain that faith until the job is done. We're like a little boy with an ice cream cone on a hot day—licking away frantically at the confection before the whole thing melts away. This is *having faith in faith*. Fortunately, God has something better in mind for us. Genuine faith, the Scriptures reveal, is a different proposition altogether.

A Lesson in Faith

Several years ago while on a ski trip with a friend in central California, I learned an interesting lesson concerning faith. After a really perfect day on the slopes, we decided to make one more run—all the way from the top. We hopped into a gondola, along with five high school girls behind us in line, and together we began the ascent to the top of majestic Mammoth Mountain. Halfway to the top, the gondola stopped—300 feet above ground. A half hour passed and, as the sun went down behind the mountain, it began to get cold. Another half hour went by and by then the gondola began swaying violently in the wind. One of the girls started to cry; another actually passed out. Things were not looking good. Suddenly, we heard a scuffling noise on the roof and a head appeared, upside down, just outside the window. It was a ski patrol who had inched his way down the cable to our aerie prison!

Producing a strap the size of a wide belt, the officer explained our means of escape: "This strap is attached by means of a cable to an automatic clutch on top of the gondola. One at a time, I want you to place the strap over your head and under your arms, and then step out the door. Don't worry; the clutch will enable you to descend slowly." A moment of silence followed as we digested this information. Then looking at me, the patrol commanded, "*You* go first."

I am a graduate of Georgia Tech and I know something about engineering. I would gladly have provided the equations governing an automatic clutch, but I did not especially want to test the efficacy of such a device. Since I had no choice, I hid my apprehensions as best I could, secured the strap as instructed, and went straight down—v-e-rry slowly. Now, believe it or not, there was faith involved in my safe landing that day. The *amount* of faith I had is not the issue. Let's just say I had enough of that commodity to actually take the steps required of me. What really saved me was the object of my faith. The automatic clutch proved reliable. It did exactly what it was supposed to do. The object of my faith was worthy of my faith.

God Is Reliable

Such is the nature of biblical faith. It is certainly not the amount of our faith that causes God to intervene on our behalf—the Lord Himself speaks of faith as small as a grain of mustard seed having the capacity to move whole mountains (Matt. 17:20). God works in our lives because He is perfectly able and willing to do that which He has promised (Rom. 4:21). God is utterly reliable. Since He has promised to direct us in the way we should go, to meet our needs, and to reward our efforts, we should take Him at His word to do so.

Abraham understood this principle well. Look at his situation 25 years after the Lord had promised that Abraham would become the father of many nations. Still childless and about 100 years of age, Abraham "contemplated his own body, now as good as dead . . . and the deadness of Sarah's womb" (Rom. 4:19). The prospect of producing a child at their ages was impossible from a human standpoint, "Yet, with respect to the promise of God, he [Abraham] did not waver in unbelief, but grew strong in faith, giving glory to God, and being fully assured that what He had promised, He was able also to perform" (4:20–21). Eventually, God honored Abraham's faith. A son was born to him from whom came "as many descendants as the stars of heaven . . . innumerable as the sand which is by the seashore" (Heb. 11:12).

When doubts assail us, we would do well to follow Abraham's example, refusing to dwell on the "impossible," choosing instead to focus on God and His Word. This does not mean we should be unrealistic regarding what is going on around us; it simply means that we need not let our circumstances get us down, for circumstances are often poor indicators of how God is working in our lives.

The New Testament gives good advice along this line: "Fixing our eyes on Jesus," is the reminder in Hebrews 12:2. In Matthew, the vivid description of Peter trying to walk across the Sea of Galilee at the command of the Master again underscores the need to keep our eyes on Jesus. Peter did fine until he looked down at the stormy sea (his circumstances). Then he began to sink. That day Peter learned a lesson about where his focus should be.

The primary truth concerning biblical faith is that it involves simply taking God at His Word and then clinging tenaciously to the object of our faith [God], regardless of circumstances.

Faith Demonstrated

A second truth concerning faith is that faith always involves action. "Faith without works is dead" (James 2:26). Another episode in the life of Abraham reflects this.

We are told that Abraham was called by God to resettle in an undesignated location far beyond the borders of his ancestral home, a location that he [Abraham] would later receive as an inheritance from God. Without hesitation, Abraham packed up his family and his belongings and "away he went, not even knowing where he was going" (Heb. 11:8, TLB).

At what point in this account did Abraham actually demonstrate his faith? When God told Abraham He had a land prepared for him, Abraham believed God. But his belief became faith when he actually moved out and took a first step toward the unknown destination. Because of his faith, God revealed to Abraham the next step of the way, and as Abraham acted on the new information, the next step was revealed, and so on.

This is typical of the way in which God works in our lives. If our response to a clear calling from God is to ask for a detailed blueprint of the whole plan, then God will probably counter with silence. But if we simply take the first step He asked of us, demonstrating our faith through action, then God will provide the information and strength needed to proceed further.

One reason that many of us do not step out in faith is that such action involves risk from a human perspective. In reality, however, the real risk lies in *not* obeying God, trusting instead in our circumstances, which are uncertain and subject to change. When we shrink in fear from a calling from God, we fail to discover the utter reliability and faithfulness of the One who sustained Abraham, and who wants to come through for us as well.

We've come a long way, haven't we, from the childish definition of faith at the beginning of this chapter. We have seen that true faith does not involve forcing ourselves to believe something we suspect is not true, but that it is based on two key elements: *belief* in the reliability of God and His Word, and *action* which is based on that belief. Combining these two elements, perhaps we can redefine faith as "acting on the conviction that God will perform what He has promised."

It is this type of faith that is called for in a partnership between God and man. Our role in such a partnership is to have faith. Nothing less on our part will do, for God has deliberately limited His ability to work in our lives without the catalyst of genuine faith.

As we consider these truths, let us not allow our lives to be like those in Nazareth where the Lord could perform no mighty works because of unbelief. Rather, let us join with God in faith and discover for ourselves that, given such a combination, nothing is impossible.

Test Yourself

At this point we should know two basic truths related to faith planning. One is that our life purpose is to glorify God by accomplishing all the unique and universal work He has given us. The second is that the way we do this is by forming a faith partnership with our Father in heaven, trusting Him to direct, provide for, and reward us as we have faith in Him.

(Personal Application, next page)

PERSONAL APPLICATION

Define biblical faith in your own words.

Faith is _____

_____

_____

_____

Identify a recent situation where you demonstrated faith by taking an action step that involved risk.

_____

_____

_____

What three things does God promise He will do in a faith-planning partnership?

_____

_____

_____

What is our part?

_____

_____

_____

4
Getting Excited about What We Don't Have

"How do you raise $200,000?" In June 1979 that question had become my major concern. After a rather tense meeting of my board of directors, it had become clear that we needed to raise $200,000—not only to accomplish our plans and dreams for the future, but even to continue the ministry of Leadership Dynamics. In all organizations, the buck must eventually stop at someone's desk. As president, I was that someone.

Over the years I have found that when I was confronted with a difficult situation, I could think more clearly when I was jogging in a wooded area. As I started down the familiar path in a favorite park near my house, a torrent of *Why* and *How* questions flooded my mind. "Lord, why me? How did I get in this situation?" I was singing the "woe is me" blues. Halfway around the park, it suddenly occurred to me, "This is an impossibility! There is no way I can do it myself." I was frightened. Then the lights went on. The Lord reminded me that I was in a partnership with Him. Besides trusting Him for my salvation, I was to trust Him for situations like this. I wasn't alone! The partnership was in place.

By the time I had circled the park, my feelings of fear and panic had been replaced by a sense of expectation and excitement that God would meet all of my needs according to His promise. I was discovering the reality of a faith goal. *A faith goal* is something we try to accomplish which requires God's direct intervention before it can be reached. To understand a faith goal, we need to build on the concept of being in a literal partnership with God. A faith goal will always have two parts—*my part* and *God's part*. My part is to exercise biblical faith and take action. God's part is to respond to my faith and, in this case, meet my specific need that His Word has promised He would.

Abraham is an example of this. "By faith Abraham, when he was called, obeyed by going out to a place which he was to receive for an inheritance; and he went out, not knowing where he was going" (Heb. 11:8). Abraham had a faith goal: to receive an inheritance. There was no way he could do it alone. He and Sarah were past the age of bearing children. Yet God had promised him an inheritance. His part (action step) was to leave Ur. God's part (area of trust) was to provide the inheritance. God fulfilled His responsibility as Abraham took his steps—one at a time.

Nothing is more exciting than to have a faith goal and see God work in specific situations in response to our steps of faith. God not only can help us accomplish great and mighty things—He wants to do so as long as we're trusting Him and giving Him the glory.

How do we establish faith goals? First, we need to identify faith areas in our lives where we have opportunities to trust God. Then we need to gain God's perspective of the situation. He does not simply respond to our every beck and call. Since "faith is the assurance of things hoped for, the conviction of things not seen" (Heb. 11:1), we need to develop the conviction that not only *can* God work in given situations, but that

He *will* work. Next we need to translate this conviction into a tangible, measurable faith-goal statement.

Opportunities to Trust God

Faith areas, then, are situations in our lives where we have opportunities to trust God. As Christians, we are to trust God generally in everything that we do, but because we are remarkably blessed in this nation as a whole, many of us do not always have occasion to trust God specifically. Much of what we need or desire comes to us simply through our efforts.

Fourteen years ago as a new Christian I heard a speaker say, "We tend to trust God only when we have to." At the time, I could not understand why that would be the case. Why wouldn't we want to trust a loving Father who cares for us? Unfortunately, over the years I've seen the truth of that statement in my own life. And I've seen it in the lives of many other Christians as well. It's called *comfortable Christianity.* Very subtly our goal becomes to live a quiet, comfortable life. If we need anything, we think that if we simply work a little harder we'll get it. God's involvement in our lives becomes strangely distant. There is little to get excited about. This is why I believe God wisely allows situations to come into our lives that we cannot handle alone. He wants us to learn to trust Him as a way of life and He uses these situations to show us His faithfulness.

Unfortunately, too many of us panic when impossible situations surface. That was my initial reaction when I was confronted with the challenge of raising $200,000. According to 1 Corinthians 10:13, we need to recognize that God allows such situations to come into our lives because He feels we are ready to handle them—but only with His help.

Our first challenge when confronted with difficult situations is to not become fearful and panic. Instead, we should get excited—excited about the opportunities to trust God specifically.

Faith areas tend to be ones where we cannot see how a goal can be reached. The Apostle Paul elaborated on this: "We look not at the things which are seen, but at the the things which are not seen; for the things which are seen are temporal, but the things which are not seen are eternal" (2 Cor. 4:18). He reminded us that we are to "walk by faith, not by sight" (2 Cor. 5:7).

The opposite of a *faith walk* is a *sight walk*. It is that desire to live a "safe" Christian life and do only what we can see.

Step Out in Faith

Noah is another in the Faith Hall of Fame. Noah was "warned by God about *things not yet seen*" (Heb. 11:7). In Noah's case the unknown was a flood. God had watered Planet Earth more through a greenhouse effect than through rain droplets. Then God told Noah it was going to rain so hard there would be a flood. Picture Noah trying to figure out what rain was all about, much less trying to understand a flood. Yet, even though Noah did not understand, he was obedient to step out in faith and prepare an ark. His part was to "build the ark for the salvation of his household." God's part was to bring the flood.

Do you have a *faith area* in your life where God is asking you to trust Him? It may not be as big as Noah's flood, but it can be just as important to you.

Several years ago after a seminar in Texas, a Christian executive shared with me how his marriage was at the point of breaking up, and he couldn't see how it could be saved. After a time of reflecting on God's character and faithfulness, his whole attitude changed. He began to see that God was giving him this unique opportunity to trust Him for his marriage.

In Minneapolis a young executive with a Christian organization needed a larger house for his growing family, but he had no financial resources to pull it off. His attitude changed from one of worry and concern to one of anticipation and excitement. He saw that he had a faith area in which he could trust his loving Father specifically.

Identifying Faith Areas

Now that we know that faith areas are opportunities in our lives to trust God specifically, let's look at two types of faith areas—needs and desires.

God has told us that He will meet our needs. This means that if a member of God's family has a need today, God is personally interested in meeting that need. Even when we are tempted to think that God is too busy to care about our needs, or that they are too small, we can reflect on this tremendous promise from God's Word.

My first encounter with this truth came shortly after I had joined the staff of Campus Crusade for Christ in 1969. The policy of the organization required each staff member to raise his own financial support base before being paid. Since my first assignment was to assist Dr. Bill Bright, the president, in some crucial reorganization needs within Campus Crusade, I was asked to forego the normal support raising time and to work on the reorganization plan. When I asked Dr. Bright what I should do about my support, he asked me if I had talked to God about my need through prayer. I had to confess that I had been too busy. Feeling the need to do something more substantial than "just praying about it," I asked him, "After I pray about it, what do I do then?" He suggested that I take one step at a time: first talk to my Father about my need and then claim His promise (Phil. 4:19).

I finally got the message. Prayer is not something you do before you do something else. It is to take priority *above* everything else. For the next four weeks, I made my need a regular part of my daily prayer life. I began to see my frustration replaced by a growing expectation. In the fifth week, I received in the mail a check for my entire first year's salary. It came from a person I had never met before! The lesson became very clear to me. God was interested in my personal needs. My responsibility was to claim His promise and trust Him to meet it.

If you have a need today, you have an opportunity to trust God. When you trust God, that pleases Him and He releases His power to meet your need. Can you see why it makes sense to get excited instead of anxious, frustrated, or upset when you have a seemingly impossible need in your life? Develop an attitude of expectation and excitement!

Desires comprise a second category of faith areas. In Psalms we read, "Delight yourself in the Lord; and He will give you the *desires* of your heart" (Ps. 37:4). I remember the first time I read that verse I couldn't believe what I was reading. It appeared to be saying that God would give me anything I wanted. My focus was on the desires. The verse suggests, however, that my focus should first be on the Lord. As I am in the process of delighting myself with Him on a daily and intimate basis, a metamorphosis takes place. His desires become my desires. I have desires, but their source is in the Lord.

Afraid to Have Desires?

The implications of Psalm 37:4 are very important in our faith-planning process. I find many Christians who are afraid to have desires, much less express them to God. Somehow they have the idea that needs are more holy and spiritual than desires. They feel they can ask God to meet their needs but not to fulfill their desires. On the contrary, Psalm 37:4 suggests that a by-product of delighting ourselves in the Lord is receiving our desires. Those who walk closest with the Lord should be the ones with great and burning desires.

Several years ago I was conducting a pastors' management

seminar in Europe. One exercise called for the pastors to write down their personal desires for the future. I noticed one pastor having a very difficult time completing the exercise. Later he came up to me and said, "I have been trying to figure out why I was not able to write down any personal desires for the future and I think I know why. I have been in the ministry for over 20 years and have been taught to suppress my personal desires and dreams—to accept more of a passive role with my church. When you asked me to write down my thoughts for the future, nothing would come out."

What a tragedy! Christians should be dreamers. If God isn't finished with His plan for earth, He is going to continue to reveal that plan to us through desires that He places in our hearts. Many of our most effective modern-day mission movements began with desires that God placed in the hearts of individuals whom He had raised up to start the jobs. A common trait of the growing and dynamic churches in America today is a desire to impact entire cities and regions of the country for Christ.

You might be thinking that it is obvious that God would lead missionaries and pastors with desires and dreams, but what about *personal* desires? What about the new house you would like to have? What about the new job? That long anticipated trip? If you are a single adult, what about a husband, a wife? I believe as long as we *first* delight ourselves in the Lord, we can get excited about personal desires. But don't get trapped into thinking that God is like the genie in the magic bottle, and that every time we have needs or desires, we simply rub the bottle and God appears to obey our every command. Those who teach that approach to planning don't understand the character and nature of God. In the next chapter, we'll deal with the importance of first determining God's perspective on our needs and desires.

PERSONAL APPLICATION

Right now God has allowed needs to come into your life. He has also given you desires. Determine what these potential faith areas are and trust Him. Begin by working through the *Identifying Faith Areas* chart which follows. Opposite each area of life are columns to indicate needs or desires that may exist now in your life. In the example on page 48, you see that *writing a book* is listed under desires as a part of the personal life, while *becoming a better father* is a need in family life. Identify your specific opportunities to trust God.

Identifying Faith Areas
Worksheet

	FAITH AREAS	
	NEEDS	**DESIRES**
AREAS OF LIFE	"And my God shall supply all your needs according to His riches in glory in Christ Jesus" (Phil. 4:19).	"Delight yourself in the Lord; and He will give you the desires of your heart" (Ps. 37:4).
PERSONAL		
FAMILY		
CHURCH		
BUSINESS VOCATIONAL		
COMMUNITY		

Identifying Faith Areas
Example

	FAITH AREAS	
	NEEDS	**DESIRES**
AREAS OF LIFE	"And my God shall supply all your needs according to His riches in glory in Christ Jesus" (Phil. 4:19).	"Delight yourself in the Lord; and He will give you the desires of your heart" (Ps. 37:4).
PERSONAL		Write a book
FAMILY	Become a better father	
CHURCH		Improve Sunday School class attendance
BUSINESS VOCATIONAL	Raise $200,000 in capital funds	
COMMUNITY		Begin a neighborhood Bible study

5
God *Will* Do It

After a seminar in the Midwest, a young man asked the question: "Now that I've identified the opportunity to trust God for a new house as a faith area, how do I know God will provide the house? I believe He *can* but I'm not sure He *will*."

This question brings us to the second part of setting faith goals. It is not enough to simply identify faith areas of needs and desires and hope that something happens. We must obtain God's perspective on them. Biblical faith requires that we not only think God *can* do it, but that we believe God *will* do it!

Several years ago I was consulting with a Christian organization sponsoring a national training conference. This conference was to be 20 times larger than any the organization had sponsored before. A small number of its top leaders had developed a conviction that God would do it, but the majority of the field leadership, which was responsible for recruiting the people to attend, believed God *could* do it but weren't sure that He *would*. They were piggybacking on the faith of others. As soon as the program was launched, problems started to surface from every direction. The reaction of the field staff was, "I wonder if this is God's will?" We are reminded in 1 Peter 1:7 that our faith will be tested as by fire. When testing comes, those without real faith (conviction) will stop, and that's what these staff members did.

Conviction Precedes Action

How many times have you launched out in a direction only to encounter trials and difficulties and wonder if this is God's will? This is why the psalmist admonished us to wait on the Lord (Ps. 37:34). Wait for His confirmation. When you have developed conviction that He will do it, then step out with confidence. This was the attitude of the Roman centurion when he said to the Lord, "Just say the word and my servant *will* be healed." Jesus marveled at this man's great faith (Matt. 8:5–10). Why? Because he really believed that Jesus would heal the servant.

How do *we* develop conviction that God will work in *our* faith areas of need or desire? The first step is to be willing to do God's will whatever it may be. Too often we come to the Lord asking Him to bless our plans. Deep inside we are already committed to a course of action and simply want the green light so we can move out. Jesus said, "If any man is willing to do His will, he shall know of the teaching, whether it is of God, or whether I speak from Myself" (John 7:17). Willingness precedes revelation. God will not give us a clear sense of direction and calling out of idle curiosity. We must first be willing to do anything He wants us to do—even if we don't want to do it.

I'd Even Go to Africa!

In January 1968 I found myself on my knees at Harvard Business School asking Christ to come into my life and to make me the kind of person that He wanted me to be. He did exactly that! My life began to change dramatically. Old desires were replaced by new ones. A hunger for God's Word replaced a desire for Friday night parties. My friends couldn't believe it and neither could I.

As the months went by, I began to wonder what God wanted me to do with my life. Then came the worst possible thought for any new Christian: "Maybe God wants me to be a *missionary*—maybe He wants me to go to Africa!" That brought stark terror to my mind. I wrestled with it for months. At the same time pressure was mounting for a career decision, but no clear signal was coming through from God.

I remember walking beside the Charles River one spring afternoon and finally agreeing to become a missionary to Africa if that was what God wanted me to do. From that point on, the fog started to lift and God began to make clear to me His will for my life. It turned out that God didn't want me to go to Africa, He simply wanted me to be *willing* to do His will above all else.

You may be in a similar situation. You desperately want something to turn out a certain way. In fact, you're outright fearful of it not turning out that way, but you have no sense of peace or conviction from God. You need simply to become *willing* for it to turn out even the opposite of how you desire it, to free up God's ability to work in your life.

My wife and I had been married for five years and the Lord had not blessed us with children, even though we had been earnestly praying for a family for three years. You can imagine our joy when in the spring of 1976 we discovered we were expecting our first child. About six months into the pregnancy, my wife's doctor had reason to believe that we were expecting twins. I remember thinking happily, "Now isn't that just like the Lord. Here we have been childless and now He is going to bless us doubly!" Tests revealed, however, that only one child was in the womb. Furthermore, the child would not live. The doctor would have to induce labor to deliver a dead baby.

I simply could not accept that. As soon as I could, I got alone with God and tried to convince Him that my will was better than His, that a live, healthy child was far preferable to this nightmarish situation we were trying to deal with. For two days and nights I pleaded, refusing to concede that God's wisdom surpassed my own in this matter. I was utterly dejected and miserable. Finally, on the third day, I reached a point at which I was honestly willing to accept God's will, whatever it might be, for this child and for any children in our future. At that moment peace and joy came over me. Even though we lost that child, we knew we were in the center of His will and experienced His comforting presence during the weeks and months that followed.

Since that difficult time, God has given us two healthy children, Brannon and Natalie. After that experience, my wife and I approached the matter of children in a different way, seeking first *God's* perspective. Both children arrived according to God's perfect timing, and both were preceded by a willingness on our part to accept God's will for our family, whatever it might be.

Developing a Vision

After we have come to a point of being willing to do God's will above everything else, we are ready to ask God to give us His vision of what He wants to do in our faith area.

Vision is picturing in our mind's eye what we believe God wants to do in our faith areas. It is "seeing" God's provision for meeting our needs, for fulfilling our desires. The Prophet Habakkuk placed a priority on obtaining God's perspective (vision) on a situation before moving out. "For the vision is yet for the appointed time; it hastens toward the goal, and it will not fail. Though it tarries, wait for it; for it will certainly come, it will not delay" (2:3). Vision enables us to turn from the seemingly impossible challenge that confronts us to the confident expectation of God's faithfulness.

Such was the case in the life of Elisha and his servant. They found themselves surrounded by the enemy Syrian army. When the servant saw the enemy horses and chariots circling the city, he ran to Elisha and exclaimed, "Master, what shall we do?" (2 Kings 6:15)

Elisha replied calmly, "Do not fear, for those who are with us are more than those who are with them" (v. 16). Then Elisha prayed a very interesting prayer: "Lord, I pray, open his eyes that he may see" (v. 17). And the Lord opened the servant's eyes to see the Lord's army outnumbering and surrounding the enemy soldiers.

What was the problem? The servant did not see God's provision. He saw only the problem. It wasn't until God opened his eyes that he saw the bigger picture and exchanged fearfulness for confidence, anxiety for calmness.

We need desperately to have our eyes opened. Too often when we are confronted with a faith area, we become paralyzed by the problem. We fail to have our inner eyes opened to God's perspective.

Vision provides the inner motivation that enables us to persevere even under the most difficult circumstances. Beginning with the Apostle Paul and his vision for preaching in Rome and beyond, church history has been marked by men and women of vision. They "saw" in the mind's eye God's plan and provision for seemingly impossible assignments. Carey saw the whole world in need of the Gospel, while others saw only their own little parishes. Henry Martyn had a vision for the Muslim world, while his church at home was engrossed in petty theological discussions.

How do we gain God's perspective on our faith areas? How

do we become persons of vision? How do we develop the mental picture of God's provision for meeting our needs?

In the life of Nehemiah we see four steps which I believe can serve as a guideline for each of us in developing a vision.

Exposure to Needs: Nehemiah, who lived approximately 450 B.C., served as cupbearer to Artaxerxes, King of Persia. It was a time of great turmoil and yet great hope for the Jewish nation. After being carried into captivity, a small band of Jews had been allowed to return to Jerusalem to lay the foundation for reestablishing Israel. Part of that foundation called for rebuilding the wall around the old city to provide a sense of security and pride for the struggling remnant.

Nehemiah inquired how the Jewish remnant which returned to Jerusalem was doing (Neh. 1:2). He discovered that they were in great distress because the wall had been broken down and the gates burned. Nehemiah found they were in need! He stumbled into a faith area because he had been willing to take the time from his schedule to be concerned with God's people and God's plans. Our purpose in life is to glorify God by accomplishing the work He has called us to do. Nehemiah was willing to interrupt his *unique* work to be concerned about God's *universal* work.

We too are challenged to be available to God's people and to identify needs. We need to avoid being trapped in our evangelical subculture, failing to see real needs all around us. I believe all visions must begin with some firsthand exposure to an area of need in which God is personally interested. Campus Crusade for Christ was born out of a vision Bill Bright had after he had immersed himself in the need to reach college students with the Gospel.

Exposure to God: When Nehemiah heard about the Jews' need, he sat down and cried for days. But that's not all he did. "I was *fasting and praying* before the God of heaven" (Neh. 1:4). Nehemiah was so distressed by the news he heard, that he talked to God for days about the problem. He didn't talk to his friend next door; he sought direct counsel from his heavenly Father.

We are prone to talk to everyone but God about needs and faith areas that come into our lives! How little time we actually spend on our knees seeking His perspective. Yet this is so essential. How can we gain God's perspective on our areas of concern without spending unhurried time with Him? We can't. After we encounter a faith area, we must spend time talking to God about it.

Exposure to the Word: Nehemiah reminded the Lord of His promise to Moses that "if you return to Me . . . I will gather them from there and will bring them to the place where I have chosen to cause My name to dwell" (Neh. 1:9). Nehemiah's vision of restoring the walled city of Jerusalem was based on a promise from God's Word. What greater confidence could Nehemiah have than to know directly from God's Word that it was His will to rebuild the wall? To have such confidence we need to know God's Word. There is no substitute. Nehemiah was able to claim God's promises because he knew God's Word. Preparing to implement a God-given vision must be preceded by time in the Scriptures.

Visualize God's Completed Work: Nehemiah's next step was to ask the king if he could return to Jerusalem and rebuild the wall. Nehemiah was able to give him a definite time frame. He requested the supplies and assistance that he would need to complete the job. How was Nehemiah able to respond in such detail when the king gave his consent? Nehemiah had formulated a picture in his mind's eye of what it would take to finish the wall and how it should look. He "saw" the completed wall before he started out on his journey.

As you are talking to God and reading His Word, visualize what God's provision for your need will look like. Mental pictures will tend to be fuzzy and general, dealing more with the "activity snapshots" that you envision as God works in your faith area. The details will be filled in later as you progress toward the goal.

A Vision for Leadership Dynamics

In 1974, while attending a series of meetings in Seoul, Korea I was impressed over and over with a desire to be truly used of God. Not knowing how to best serve His purposes, I went to my room during one of the breaks, got down on my knees and asked God to show me any task in the world He would have me accomplish, even if it was one nobody else would take on. During the next several weeks, the Lord began to give me a picture of a unique training ministry. The ministry I envisioned was essentially for Christian business and professional people, and was designed to help equip these people to manage and lead in their various spheres of influence, according to biblical principles.

My original vision became more distinct as I spent quality time with the Lord. Eventually I began to meet with a select group of men who were equally challenged by the vision. It was from these discussions of how to make the vision a reality that our present ministry, Leadership Dynamics International, was born. Though a lot of hard work has gone into the forming and managing of this organization, I have never forgotten that it all started with a simple vision from God, a picture of what He wanted me to do in my area of faith.

The last step in developing the "assurance of things hoped for, the conviction of things not seen" (Heb. 11:1) is to wait on the Lord to confirm His leading. David reminded us: "Wait for the Lord; be strong, and let your heart take courage; yes, wait for the Lord" (Ps. 27:14).

Mental pictures come and go. Sometimes we have a difficult time discerning between God's leading and our leading. Visions can be simply emotional responses to areas of need. You and I need God's confirmation that He is the source of our visions. We need a "stake in the ground" experience that we can refer back to when the going gets tough.

Three Tests

I believe that there are three tests that will help us discern whether or not our vision is, in fact, God's leading. First there's the test of time. Does the vision grow or does it die? God's calling will intensify over time, while our purely emotional leadings will fade away. That's why it is important not to rush quickly into a new vision venture until we've let some time go by. Our problem is that we live in a *now* generation. We want instant meals (with microwave ovens) and instant cures (with miracle drugs). The philosophy of instant gratification has imbedded itself into our relationship with the Lord. We want instant conviction. It doesn't happen that way; it takes time. I began Leadership Dynamics two years after the original vision. During this "perk time," the vision grew and intensified.

Another test is through our thoughts. We read in 1 Corinthians that we have the mind of Christ (2:16). Our sanctified minds being renewed by God's Word through His Spirit can also become a source of confirmation (Rom. 12:3). When we are walking closest with the Lord, what comes into our minds? When we have quality quiet times with Him, what surfaces in our thinking? I believe that if visions are from the Lord, we can expect them to spill over in our thought lives as we walk with Him.

A third test revolves around the peace we feel. As time goes by and the vision intensifies, as we think about our visions during our closest walks with the Lord, do we experience a sense of peace? If we do, I believe this is a further confirmation of God's leading. "Wisdom will enter your heart, and knowledge will be pleasant to your soul" (Prov. 2:10). In

Colossians we read, "Let the *peace* of Christ rule in your hearts" (3:15).

My decision to step out and begin the ministry of Leadership Dynamics was accompanied by much fear and trembling, but I could always point back to a time when I knew that God had given me His peace in implementing the vision.

When you experience His peace about the vision He has given you, drive your stake in the ground. Write down the date of His confirmation. Let this be the gyroscope to govern and control your future actions as you take steps to see the vision become a reality.

PERSONAL APPLICATION

Select *one* faith area from the *Identifying Faith Areas* chart (page 47). Be sure it is one that you want to work on. Enter it on the *Faith-Planning* chart on the next page. Then, visualize God's provision for meeting that need or desire in the next section. Take time to be alone with the Lord, seeking His confirmation of the vision. When He gives you the conviction that He will do it, write the date on the line provided. My example of raising $200,000 is shown on the sample *Faith-Planning* chart immediately following the worksheet.

Faith-Planning Chart
Worksheet

Faith Area   An area of need, concern, or desire in my life is:

_____

_____

Vision   In my mind's eye I see the following activities taking place as God works in my faith area:

_____

_____

_____

_____

_____

_____

Confirmation   On this date I have a conviction that this is what God wants to do:

_____

Faith-Planning Chart
Example

Faith Area   An area of need, concern, or desire in my life is:

Business/vocational life: Raise $200,000 in capital

funds

Vision   In my mind's eye I see the following activities taking place as God works in my faith area:

Expansion of our ministry throughout the country

Pastors being trained in leadership principles

Ongoing training centers in cities where executives are

taught biblical principles of management

Churches establishing regular training classes to

better equip their church leaders

Confirmation   On this date I have a conviction that this is what God wants to do:

July 30

6
Putting the Faith Partnership to Work

After isolating the faith areas in our lives and establishing conviction that God will work in those areas, we are ready for phase three: setting the goals. Perhaps you are wondering why goals are necessary. Isn't it enough that we have a God-given course of action in our mind's eyes? Not if we want to function as effectively as possible.

Goals Provide Direction
The beauty of goals is that they give direction to our activities, enabling us to realize the greatest possible return on our investment of time and energy. What's more, goals enable us to exercise good stewardship of our God-given resources. Without goals, we may find ourselves spending a lot of time in activity that yields little in terms of accomplishment or fulfillment.

A goal is a phenomenon that needs to be distinguished from a mere good intention which I like to call a fuzzy. A *fuzzy* is a vague, generalized project or activity that we have every intention of accomplishing, but since it is largely undefined, we have no way of measuring our progress as we work on it. And we are never quite sure when it is finished.

A *goal*, on the other hand, is a precise target. It is a clear-cut, well-defined intention that has a definite beginning and a definite end. A goal enables us to measure our progress every step of the way, and when we have completed the designated task, we will know it.

I discovered firsthand the pitfalls of a fuzzy as I attempted to "become a better husband." After a couple of months of working on that rather vague intention, I turned to my wife one evening and commented on how great it was that I was becoming such a good husband. I was deflated when Donna replied, "Honey, I think it's wonderful that you're trying, but I really don't see much progress." I had imagined that I was getting somewhere, but in reality, things weren't that much different than before. I should have translated my good intention into a series of concrete, tangible goals such as: "Spend one evening a week with Donna in fellowship and relaxation, beginning on September 1."

On September 2, I would know whether I was making progress, and on December 2, I would know whether or not I had reached my goal. A true goal is measurable and attainable.

Faith Goals
Now that we know the difference between a goal and a fuzzy, let's look at what it is that differentiates an ordinary goal from a faith goal. An ordinary goal is based on the resources at hand, while a *faith goal* is based on a working partnership with God.

When setting goals for ourselves the temptation is to fall into the trap of projection planning (discussed in chapter one) and to base those goals on what has happened in the past and the resources currently at hand. If we follow this procedure, we will come up with goals of the ordinary variety, and we will miss the opportunity to see God work miraculously in our lives. On the other hand, if we base our goals on the vision God has given us, our hopes will be realized to an extent beyond imagining. We will begin to experience the reality of Paul's words to the Ephesians: "Now to Him who is able to do exceeding abundantly beyond all that we ask or think, according to the power that works within us" (3:20).

Several years ago, my wife and I decided to test this principle in relation to a Bible study we wanted to hold in our Atlanta neighborhood. Our vision was to make an impact on the *entire* neighborhood through the study of God's Word. That fall, we and another Christian couple began to set our goals. We were tempted to aspire to a study for just three or four couples. This, we figured, was a realistic goal, considering we could probably drum up that many ourselves from among the 100 or so couples around us. Furthermore, since no study currently existed, three or four couples studying the Word would represent a 300 to 400 percent increase over the status quo, which was pretty good.

The scope of our vision, however, was for our entire neighborhood of approximately 100 homes. We decided, then, that the basis of our faith goal should be a number which would move us toward the total scope of our vision—not merely an increase over the past. After praying about it, we arrived at the faith goal of 20 couples committed to attend a study beginning January 1.

Too often, we Christians tend to put ceilings on what we feel we can ask of God, and yet Jesus continually admonished His disciples to *ask*. We have the scriptural promise that whatever we ask, believing, we will receive. We can believe that we'll receive what we ask for if we have the *conviction* that what we're asking for is firmly rooted in God's will.

You might be thinking, "What about Jesus' remarks, 'For

which one of you, when he wants to build a tower, does not first sit down and calculate the cost, to see if he has enough to complete it?' " (Luke 14:28) This verse does not contradict the concept of planning by faith, but rather advises us to be fully and realistically aware of what is actually involved in reaching our goals. When we know our needs in terms of time, talent, and treasure, we can ask God specifically for help in meeting those needs, remembering that God has *promised* to come through for us as we seek His will (Rom. 4:21).

A friend of mine related to me an experience he had while raising funds for an evangelistic organization. He approached an extremely wealthy businessman in the Christian community and rather timidly asked for a contribution of $5,000. The man said, "Certainly," and wrote out a check in the specified amount. Some time later, my friend discovered that the very next day that same businessman graciously handed out a check for $50,000, simply because that was the amount asked for by another worthwhile organization. My friend's elation over the $5,000 gift turned to disappointment as he realized he could have raised a far greater sum for his cause had he *asked* for it. A hard lesson, perhaps, but one that we would all do well to remember in our dealings with God.

God's Part and My Part

Since a faith goal is built on a partnership basis with God, it must be readily divisible into two parts—God's part and my part. God's part identifies my specific area of trust and my part identifies the specific action I will take. This again ties back to the two characteristics of biblical faith—trust in God and His Word, and action.

We see this principle in the lives of Noah and Abraham. Noah's faith goal was to save his family from the upcoming Flood and to be the source of repopulating Planet Earth. God's part was to bring the Flood. There was no way Noah could produce a flood through his own efforts. That became an area of trust. His part was to build the ark. Noah received specific instructions on how to build the ark. This is what God asked him to do. So Noah did his part and God performed His part.

Abraham was trusting God for the inheritance. Abraham's part was to leave Ur. As Abraham left Ur, God began to show him the next steps he should take.

MY PART	GOD'S PART
Noah: Build the Ark	Bring the Flood
Abraham: Leave Ur	Provide the inheritance

If you write a faith goal and find there is nothing to put under the *God's Part* column on your paper, you really don't have a faith goal.

A case in point was a church in Tennessee whose finance committee determined to set up a faith goal pertaining to the budget for the coming year. As the committee members were working with their planning sheet, they discovered to their surprise that all the activities necessary to realize the goal fell under the *My Part* column. In other words, they were planning to trust in their own resources rather than in God.

Eventually, the committee rewrote its goal, this time including God in the plans. Under the *God's Part* column were the words: To work in the hearts of the church members so that the budget might be raised in 45 days instead of in the normal six months of canvassing and arm-twisting.

At the end of the 45 days, I received a letter from the committee informing me that 98 percent of the budget had come in, breaking all previous records. They were excited! Each was experiencing the rewards of reaching a faith goal through a true partnership with God.

Focus on God's Resources
As you go about the task of setting a faith goal of your own, ask yourself this question: "If resources were no problem,

what would I see being accomplished in my faith area (based on what God has shown me as His will), and when would I see it happen?"

This question is designed to help you focus on God's resources rather than your own, and to help you make your goal specific—measurable and attainable, as opposed to fuzzy. Once you have set the goal, write it out in full and then divide your goal into two parts: *My Part* and *God's Part,* listing under each part the appropriate responsibilities.

When I identified the faith goal to raise $200,000 in six weeks for Leadership Dynamics, I wrote my goal on paper, and then made two distinct columns on the page. Heading one of the columns were the words: *God's Part.* Heading the other were the words: *My Part.* Under the column entitled *My Part,* I wrote the following: To contact 50 individuals who had been involved in the ministry of Leadership Dynamics and who had the financial capacity to give. Under *God's Part,* I wrote: To raise up interested people and motivate them to give. The pressure was suddenly off when I realized that it wasn't my job to do the convincing. That was God's responsibility. My responsibility was simply to share the need and trust God for the results.

MY PART	GOD'S PART
Call 50 people	Positive responses

Excited at the prospect of working on a faith goal, I called the first person on the list. He said he would pray about it. The second person was out of town. The third person had already given his quota for the year to Christian organizations. I couldn't reach the fourth person. The fifth person said he was not interested. I was wiped out!

I said to God, "Here I am, trying to follow a faith plan. I'm doing my part; why aren't You doing Yours?" My answer came in the form of a still, small voice that said, "Bruce, how many people have you called?"

"Five," I answered meekly.

"How many were you supposed to call?"

"Fifty," I replied.

By the time I had called 50 people, the entire sum was raised—though not the way I had anticipated. The Lord declared, "My thoughts are not your thoughts, neither are your ways My ways" (Isa. 55:8).

We can never determine *how* God will do His part. What is under God's column, forget about. He will perform His part in His own special way, and in His own good time. We are simply to concentrate on the tasks at hand, giving them the best that we have and resting secure in the knowledge that God *will* perform what He has promised.

PERSONAL APPLICATION

Your challenge now is to translate your vision from the worksheet on page 59 into a specific faith goal. First, rewrite your vision statement from page 59 to the top portion of the faith-planning chart on the next page. Next ask yourself the question: "If resources were no problem, what specific goal would I want to accomplish and by when?" In the example of *beginning a neighborhood Bible study* (page 70), the faith goal becomes *beginning a Bible study for 10 couples by January 1.* Where did the number 10 come from? It was from the *scope of the vision* which was to impact the *entire* neighborhood. A projection goal would have been merely content to increase what was already going on. A faith goal will always have its basis in the vision. After writing your faith goal, the last step is to divide it into two parts—*my part* and *God's part.* Refer to the two examples provided on pages 69 and 70 as you complete your Faith-Planning Chart.

Faith-Planning Chart
Worksheet

Faith Area   An area of need, concern, or desire in my life is:

_____

_____

Vision   In my mind's eye I see the following activities taking place as God works in my faith area:

_____

_____

_____

_____

_____

Confirmation   On this date I have a conviction that this is what God wants to do:

_____

Faith Goal   If resources were no problem, what specific goal would I want to accomplish and by when?

_____

_____

_____

_____

My Part (Area of Action)   **God's Part** (Area of Trust)

_____   _____

_____   _____

_____   _____

Faith-Planning Chart
Example 1

Faith Area   An area of need, concern, or desire in my life is:

BUSINESS/VOCATIONAL LIFE: Raise $200,000 in

capital funds.

Vision   In my mind's eye I see the following activities taking place as God works in my faith area:

Expansion of our ministry throughout the country

Pastors being trained in leadership principles

Ongoing training centers in cities where executives are taught biblical principles of management

Churches establishing regular training classes to better train and equip their church leaders

Confirmation   On this date I have a conviction that this is what God wants to do.

October 1st

Faith Goal   If resources were no problem, what specific goal would I want to accomplish and by when?

Raise 200,000 by March 30.

My Part (Area of Action)

Make a list of potential investors and challenge them to invest

God's Part (Area of Trust)

Provide the investors

Faith-Planning Chart
Example 2

Faith Area   An area of need, concern, or desire in my life is:

COMMUNITY: Begin a neighborhood Bible study.

Vision   In my mind's eye I see the following activities taking place as God works in my faith area:

Neighbors becoming Christians and being built up in their faith

Lives and families being changed

A new atmosphere of love and sharing in our neighborhood

Confirmation   On this date I have a conviction that this is what God wants to do:

October 1st

Faith Goal   If resources were no problem, what specific goal would I want to accomplish and by when?

Begin an evangelistic Bible study for 20 neighborhood

couples by January 1.

My Part (Area of Action)	**God's Part** (Area of Trust)
1. Contact other Christian core couples to cosponsor the study.	1. Raise up at least two other Christian couples.
2. Contact and invite non-Christian neighbors.	2. Cause the non-Christian neighbors to want to attend.

7
How God Precedes Us

A pastor came to me following a seminar and expressed a lament common to many Christians. "Setting faith goals is not my problem," he said. "I've set faith goals all my life. What I can't do is actually reach one." Anyone who has successfully reached a faith goal knows that it is not enough to simply have the goal. We must also have an effective means of reaching the goal. We need a *faith strategy.*

Faith strategy answers the question of *how* we do our part in reaching the faith goal, and becomes the third step in the faith-planning ladder. Even though it is *My Part* of the faith goal we are working on, it is important to realize that God is with us every step of the way as we seek to do His will in the faith-planning process. If we know that God has called us to a specific faith goal, we can know that He has preceded us with a specific strategy as well.

God will lay the groundwork necessary for the best strategy to evolve. We must discover how God has preceded us and take advantage of it. A story from the Old Testament illustrates this point.

God Preceded Gideon

At a certain point during the period of Judges in Israel's history, God's people were cruelly oppressed by the conquering Midianite army. Eventually, the Lord charged Gideon, a farmer's son, with an enormous faith goal: "Go," said the Lord, "and deliver Israel from the hand of Midian" (Jud. 6:14).

Stunned by such a directive, Gideon proceded to set out a fleece (literally in this case) to determine whether the prescribed mission was really God's will. When he became convinced that it was, Gideon found himself in desperate need of a strategy. His first approach to the challenge was to gather together all the resources he could muster, eventually coming up with an army of 32,000 (not very large compared with the Midianite army which numbered 135,000). Through a series of circumstances, however, God reduced the army to a mere 300 men "Lest," as the Lord explained, "Israel become boastful, saying, 'My own power has delivered me' " (Jud. 7:2).

Can you relate to Gideon's experience? Have you ever tackled a faith goal by gathering together all your own resources in terms of time, people, and money, only to have them stripped away in midcourse? I have, and such a development leads to immense frustration. Perhaps the Lord was reminding you, as He was Gideon, and as He has me on several occasions, that our dependence should be on Him and on Him alone.

What was Gideon to do with his resources cut back to 300 men? I'm afraid that many well-meaning Christians today would go for a frontal approach, attacking at high noon with the little band of men. After all, they might reason, it was God who gave the command in the first place, and He has promised to see His own will through to completion. True, but God is not in the habit of underwriting brash and ill-conceived action. Rather, He requires that "all things be done properly and in an orderly manner" (1 Cor. 14:40).

Fortunately, for everyone involved, Gideon learned in time that his best course would be to determine how God had preceded him. So that Gideon might develop his strategy, God sent him on a reconaissance mission into the enemy camp. There Gideon overheard a soldier describing a dream he had had in which the Midianite army was thoroughly routed. Gideon observed that the soldier and all his company were consumed with fear because of the dream. Recognizing the new turn of events as the Lord's handiwork, Gideon developed a clever strategy to take advantage of the fear his enemy felt. This is what Gideon did:

> He divided the 300 men into three companies, and he put trumpets and empty pitchers into the hands of all of them, with torches inside the pitchers. And he said to them, "Look at me, and do likewise. And behold, when I come to the outskirts of the camp, do as I do. When I and all who are with me blow the trumpet, then you also blow the trumpets all around the camp, and say, 'For the Lord and for Gideon. . . .' " When they blew 300 trumpets, the Lord set the sword of one against another even throughout the whole army, and the army fled (Jud. 7:16–18, 22).

Gideon had reached his goal! He had delivered Israel from the hand of Midian, just as he had been instructed. In the process he learned that the most awesome of faith goals can be reached by determining how God has preceded us in our efforts. The groundwork that God laid for Gideon had to do with fear, but the groundwork he lays for us is as varied as the different goals to which we aspire.

God Precedes Missionaries

In his book *Peace Child* (Regal), Don Richardson contends that God has paved the way for sharing the Gospel in every culture in the world by placing within that culture some analogy to the

Gospel story. When we discover that analogy, we can make the Gospel understood and reach our goal of winning others for Christ.

A case in point involves Richardson's experiences on a remote South Seas Island where he was once sent as a missionary. The tribe native to the island was part of a topsy-turvy culture in which treachery and deceit were highly valued, and such qualities as truth and honesty were considered foolish. The tribesmen actually applauded *Judas* when author Don Richardson shared with them Judas' role in the Gospel story.

Richardson was getting nowhere in his missionary efforts until he discovered one day that at the conclusion of every major skirmish the kings of the tribes involved would exchange sons so that each would be loathe to wage further war against the other. A light went on. Using this unorthodox practice as an analogy, Richardson was able to explain that the King of the world sent His only Son to live among us so that we might have peace through His death on the cross. The message got through and, eventually, every one of the tribesmen Richardson was trying to reach chose to follow Christ.

Richardson's situation was out of the ordinary, and so was the way in which God preceded him. More commonly, God precedes us by placing a need in the heart of the person or group we are trying to influence. By discovering that need and meeting it, we are able to accomplish the goal. We call this a *felt need* because the person or group we are trying to influence feels this need and it is a growing priority in their lives.

Jesus Met a Felt Need
Another illustration of this concept is the story of Jesus and the woman at the well. The Samaritan woman felt that she needed water, so Jesus assisted her in her efforts to get it.

Once Jesus had the woman's full attention, He was able to speak to her about her *real need* for spiritual water.

When my wife and I were making plans for the neighborhood Bible study, we knew that very few of our neighbors felt any real need for a weekly study of God's Word. They did, however, feel a need to socialize, especially during the holidays; so we held a "real meaning of Christmas" party in our home. Of the 50 couples who attended, 20 signed up for the study after we had shared our testimonies and described what the study would be like. By meeting our neighbors' felt needs for socializing, we were to be able to help meet their real needs for spiritual nourishment, thereby reaching our goal.

Another example of how the Lord precedes us in our efforts is on a much grander scale, but the principle is the same. In 1970, the leadership of Campus Crusade for Christ set a goal to recruit 100,000 individuals as delegates to Explo '72, a week-long training event to be held in Dallas, Texas in June of 1972. The sessions were designed to equip participants with the motivation and skills to engage in personal evangelism and discipleship. By January 1972, only 3,000 persons had registered, and this number included the staff members of Campus Crusade. We were in big trouble, as hotel rooms had already been booked, speakers lined up, and the Cotton Bowl reserved. Prayerfully (and quickly), we revised our recruitment strategy, which had been directed at individuals, and began to seek delegations from schools and churches to attend Explo. This strategy worked, for on the eve of the big event 85,000 young people and adults had registered. We were delighted (and relieved). By meeting a felt need to be part of a delegation group (attending a major happening with friends), we were going to be able to meet a largely *unfelt* need for evangelistic training, thereby reaching our goal.

Be Sure to Ask

As we go about the development of a faith strategy, we would do well to bear in mind three directives: "*Ask,* and it shall be given to you; *seek,* and you shall find; *knock,* and it shall be opened to you" (Luke 11:9). Notice that each directive is followed by a promise.

We are instructed to ask. What we need to ask for in this case is the wisdom to determine how God has preceded us with plans for a strategy. The promise of Luke 11:9 that we will receive what we ask for is reinforced in James: "If any of you lacks wisdom, let him *ask* of God, who gives to all men generously and without reproach, and it *will* be given to him" (1:5).

We are instructed to seek. The object of our search is to determine how God has preceded us through placing felt needs in the hearts of those with whom we are trying to work.

Gideon had to leave his "council of war" meeting and actually infiltrate the enemy camp in order to discover how God had preceded him. This is a detail worth noting. I have seen many seemingly excellent strategies fail because they were based on what the planners *thought* would influence people rather than on how the Lord had actually preceded them at the grass-roots level.

Such procedure is known as *top-down planning,* and it simply does not work in relation to a faith goal. God's groundwork, though not excessively obscure, requires a search; that is, we generally must look beyond our own noses to find it. The best way to conduct the search is to survey or talk directly to the people we are trying to influence. Let them tell us what their needs are.

A well-intended strategy of a Christian organization went astray because of a failure to do this. They produced a film that they reasoned would appeal to non-Christians and could be used to reach them with the Gospel. After spending months in production and in excess of $1 million, the film bombed when it hit the secular market. In Atlanta, it closed after one night's running.

What went wrong? Was it not God's will that people be reached through the film? Did the planners not discern God's leading? I think their error was, very simply, lack of identifying how God had preceded them. They *assumed* the film and its title would appeal to a non-Christian audience. What should they have done? They should have surveyed their prospective audience and determined what *felt needs* existed that they could build on in producing and promoting the film.

Unfortunately, this scenario is reproduced too often within the Christian community. Consequently, well-intentioned projects for the Lord run aground because of the lack of a *need*-oriented strategy.

Basis for Strategy

As you attempt to determine how God has preceded you in your own faith goal, ask yourself these questions: "*Who*, specifically, am I trying to influence? *What* must the person or group that I am trying to influence *do* (purchase a ticket, sign up for a course, donate a sum of money, etc.) in order for my goal to be reached?" Then ask: "*Why* would a person want to do that (felt need)?" When you discover what it is that will motivate an individual to action, you will see the groundwork God has laid for you, and this should be the basis for your strategy. The answers to these three questions become the *critical events* of your strategy and will ultimately determine success or failure. If there is not a positive response to the *why* question, you have not yet determined how God has preceded you and your strategy probably will not work.

The third directive in the command is to knock. Once we have determined to the best of our abilities how it is that God has preceded us and developed a strategy to take advantage of His groundwork, we need to stop mulling over our decision and get on with implementing it. Some of us are perpetual seekers, unable to put our plans into action for fear that we might fail, or that we have mistaken God's calling. Look again at Gideon, our biblical example. Gideon could have allowed himself to be paralyzed by the thought of his little band lighting its torches and blowing its trumpets before the mighty Midianites; instead, he trusted in the strategy God had given him, and he went through with it. Until we knock, or actually step out, the door to success will remain tightly closed. Again we see the risk element of faith planning. Yet the risk is only from a human perspective. There is no risk in trusting God.

PERSONAL APPLICATION

Review the example for determining critical events (page 80). In encouraging investors to contribute to our ministry, the *who* and *what* was getting one investor to contribute $10,000. *Why* would he want to do that? After I talked with some of the potential investors, there appeared to be three felt needs that I could build on in doing my part:

1. As businessmen, they were all interested in seeing good returns on their contributions.

2. They were interested in personally helping me because of the relationships we had established.

3. They had attended our seminars and had developed a need to see other Christian executives exposed to the same life-changing principles.

In beginning a neighborhood Bible study, the *who* and *what* became getting one couple from our neighborhood to attend a Bible study. Answering the question *why* required identifying in more detail the demographics of our neighborhood. Many of the couples were older and were experiencing a sense of alienation and aloneness; therefore, we surmised that their felt need might be social and we could build on that. An invitation to our study should present the opportunity to meet and to become better acquainted with other couples in the neighborhood.

On the worksheet chart on page 81, write your faith goal in the first column. Next, identify *who* the person or group is that you are trying to influence. Determine *what* they must do, and *why* they would do it. The answers to these three questions will give you your critical event.

Determining Critical Events
Example

FAITH GOAL	WHO?	WHAT?	WHY?
To begin a neighborhood Bible study	A neighborhood couple	To attend an evangelistic Bible study	Social needs (get to know neighbors better) Relationship with sponsoring couple
To raise $200,000	An LDI alumni with a gift of giving	Invest $10,000	Personal relationship Committed to LDI vision Good return on investment

Determining Critical Events
Worksheet

FAITH GOAL	WHO?	WHAT?	WHY?

8
Stepping Out
on the Faith Limb

Since introducing faith planning, we have looked at understanding the life purpose of the Christian (glorifying God through
the work we have been called to do in a partnership relationship with Him); establishing faith goals (discovering the faith
areas in our lives and developing a vision of what the Lord
wants us to do in those areas); and developing a faith strategy
(discovering how the Lord has preceded us and developing a
strategy to take advantage of His groundwork).

Implement the Strategy
We are ready to deal with the fourth and final step in the
faith-planning process: implementing the strategy so we can
actually reach our goals.

To do this we need to translate our strategy into simple
steps or activities that will serve to get us from Point A
(where we are now) to Point B (where we want to go). Then
we need to schedule our activities in time; write them out in
logical sequence on a calender or chart. Finally, we need to
engage in the activities we have scheduled. Until we begin to

move out, our goals will remain mere good intentions waiting to be fulfilled.

Translating Strategy into Steps

The story of Gideon shows us how these implementation steps take place. Gideon came up with a strategy which was based on the fear God had implanted in the hearts of the conquering Midianites. To follow through with his plan, Gideon first had to translate that strategy into specific activities, which on paper might have looked something like this:

Divide men into three companies of 100 each

Provide men with supplies: pitchers, candles, trumpets

Issue instructions

Attack Midianite army

Obviously, much more detail was involved in Gideon's plans, but you get the picture. Then Gideon had to schedule his activities. He had to decide when he was going to carry out each one. Finally, he actually had to perform the activities, starting with number one and continuing down his list until the final activity was completed.

Implementing the Bible-Study Plan

My wife and I followed much the same format as we set about to implement our strategy for the neighborhood Christmas party. First, we translated our strategy into specific activities such as:

Decide on a speaker and ask him to speak

Get names and addresses of everyone in neighborhood

Purchase invitations

Write invitations

Mail invitations

Prepare refreshments

Line up chairs for evening

We scheduled all the activities we had come up with on our

calendar and then set about doing them one by one, until our goal was reached.

I could end the chapter here and wish you well in your own endeavors, if what I have explained were all there was to a faith strategy, but in reality there is often a twist involved. In the course of implementing any faith strategy, a hindrance of some sort usually arises and threatens to throw us off course.

For Moses, it was the Red Sea (and later the rebellion of the people he was trying to help) that were deterrents; for Paul, it was whippings, shipwrecks, beatings, and robberies that threatened to undermine his efforts to establish the church throughout the Roman Empire. In the case of Gideon, 15,000 of the dreaded Midianites managed to escape from the fray causing Gideon all sorts of unexpected difficulties. (To see how Gideon resolved his dilemma, turn to Judges 7 and 8.)

Why Twists?

Why is it that we often encounter plan-threatening barriers when we are pursuing what God has revealed to be His will? The answer to this problem is twofold. First, we read in the Scriptures that we are tested in order that our faith might be proven, and thereby bring glory to our Lord Jesus Christ (1 Peter 1:7). The testing of our faith produces endurance, a quality that we need in order to become ultimately "perfect and complete, lacking in nothing" (James 1:3-4).

God allows the troublesome barriers to surface in our lives, and since the end results are beneficial (God is glorified and our own characters have a chance to become ultimately perfected), we are told that we can actually "consider it all joy ... when [we] encounter various trials"! (James 1:2) Though they are beneficial, barriers do constitute a definite nuisance in our lives and they need to be worked through. How do we overcome the barriers that so readily threaten success?

First, we need to develop *attitudes of endurance* so that

when the going gets rough we don't simply buckle under and give up.

I learned a valuable personal lesson in endurance when I was a freshman at Georgia Tech. I had enrolled in Physical Education 101 thinking it would be the snap course I needed to offset some really difficult math and science courses I was taking. As it turned out, however, Phys. Ed. 101, which was designed to "drown-proof" its enrollees, was a veritable bone crusher. We students were expected to come through the course equipped with the skill and the confidence to handle any water-related mishap that might befall us.

For instance, one exercise was to tie our hands behind our backs, simulating the fact that our arms had cramped up. Then we were asked, as a class, to jump into the water, to swim with a dolphin kick down to the end of an Olympic-size pool, let out our air, sink to the bottom of the pool, grasp a plastic ring in our teeth, and surface. When we surfaced, we had to swim one width of the pool under water. If we did all of that, we got an A. If we didn't complete the underwater swim, we got a B. If we didn't quite get the ring in our mouth, we got a C. If we didn't make it down to the deep end of the pool, we got a D. If we didn't do the exercise at all, we got an F.

After weeks of grueling exercises that made math and science seem like child's play, our instructor introduced a real killer known simply as the underwater swim. We were asked to swim two lengths of the Olympic-size pool underwater. It is a feat which can apparently be accomplished by only 6 percent of the nation's freshmen. But 60 percent of Georgia Tech freshmen were victorious. Our coach was extremely proud of this fact, to say the least.

To motivate us beyond what we normally were able to achieve, that same coach assembled all 75 of us at the end of the pool one day and announced that if all of us were able to complete the swim, we would get an *A* for the course, regardless of our previous records. If even one of us were to fail, however, the deal would be off. One after another the students made the swim until, amazingly, almost two-thirds of the class had successfully completed the assignment. Then it was my turn—and I was faced with one of the most difficult decisions of my college days. I had never made the swim before, but I determined that I would die underwater if necessary rather than emerge prematurely and die at the hands of my classmates, who would surely kill me if I soured the deal.

Learning Endurance

I took the plunge, completed my somersault (meant to simulate the disorientation one might feel after a car accident), and headed off. I first thought that I hadn't gotten enough air, but I kept going. I began to experience increasing discomfort, and by the time I reached the two-thirds mark on the pool, every cell in my body was screaming out that I could endure no more. I remembered the coach pointing to this place in the water earlier and warning us that such a sensation often occurs at the two-thirds mark of the pool, but if we would force ourselves to take *one more stroke,* we could get through the barrier and be on our way.

I made myself take one more stroke and then discovered that I could take one more, and then another, until I found myself at the end of the pool. I kicked off and began the long haul back and, sure enough, at the two-thirds mark, I again had the sensation that my lungs would explode. I made myself take another stroke, and then another, and eventually, miracle of miracles, I had completed the run.

Now I wish I could tell you that each of us in the class made an *A* that semester, but, unfortunately, the student directly behind me in line became confused during his somersault, swam toward the wrong end of the pool and surfaced as his head hit the side. The deal was off.

While I didn't get a good grade in the course, I did learn the lesson of perserverance. I discovered firsthand the payoff of an attitude that says, "I'm not coming up. I'm going to take one more stroke, one more stroke."

When barriers impede our progress as we are implementing a faith strategy, we may be tempted to give up or to assume that we are in pursuit of the wrong goals. Instead, we must remember the benefits of perserverance and ask God to give us the strength to take *one more step*. The next step will be easier, and eventually we will have accomplished what we set out to do. One of my favorite verses is, "For you have need of endurance, so that when you have done the will of God, you may receive what was promised" (Heb. 10:36). Endurance is the key to implementing a faith goal.

Remain Flexible

A second point to remember in overcoming barriers is to remain flexible to make needed midcourse corrections. The ability to make these corrections will determine whether many faith goals are ever reached. Let me share with you another personal example from involvement in Explo '72.

When the Dallas hotels in which we were holding rooms found out that only 3,000 of an anticipated 100,000 delegates had registered by January, they understandably requested that we either cancel the rooms or come up with a deposit for each of them. We didn't have the money for the deposits, so, regrettably, we had to let most of the rooms go.

Then when we changed our recruiting strategy and began to seek delegations, thousands of additional delegates were recruited during the last months before the conference. The upshot of this new development was that we had the delegates but we didn't have the rooms, and we needed 50,000 of them.

Prayerfully, we came up with a strategy to accommodate the thousands of people we were expecting: We would ask our staff to go door to door in the Dallas area and challenge people individually to open their homes to our high school and college students. We figured that the hospitality of these Texans would come through, that they would want to help us in such a way. As it turned out, many of them did; but at the end of several week's endeavors, we were still short 40,000 beds. We realized that in light of our approaching deadline, we had to alter our strategy and try something else. *Plan A* simply was not bearing enough fruit.

Our next course of action was to run full-page ads in the Dallas newspapers, featuring photos of sharp, clean-cut students holding suitcases. Accompanying each photo was the caption, "No Place to Stay," an explanation of what the students would be doing in Dallas, and a telephone number at which those willing to open their homes for the week could reach us. So far, so good. But when one of the first calls to come in was from a strange-sounding fellow requesting three high school girls, we realized, to our horror, that we had no feasible way to screen the calls. So much for *Plan B.*

Now it so happened that at the time we lost our hotel rooms, we had considered using empty apartment units for accommodations, but had scrapped the idea when we learned that no one would insure us against possible damages. Now we decided to go back to the insurance companies and ask again—*Plan C.* Only three weeks remained. As we entered the office of the insurance executive, we were greeted more cordially than we had expected, and after we had made our request known for the second time, he replied, "You know, if you had come one week earlier, I would have turned you down again, but my daughter has been in a serious automobile accident since then. She was looking forward to attending Explo '72 and now that she can't go, I would like to make it possible for others to attend. I'll write whatever policy you need."

To say that we were thrilled to have our problem resolved would be to grossly understate our feelings. We gave copies of the policy to our teams, who took them to the apartment managers who, in turn, allowed us to lease the units we required. When the delegates arrived, each had a place to stay. The Dallas papers commended us on our excellent management of the event. They knew nothing about the behind-the-scenes endurance and the midcourse corrections.

Dealing with Barriers

As any faith strategy is being implemented, we can be sure that one or more barriers will arise and threaten to wreak havoc with our well-laid plans. We can get through those barriers if we remember these principles:

Endurance: Don't give up, for God has promised to be with us every step of the way in the entire faith planning process. We must ask Him to give the strength to take just one more step, and then another, until we have actually accomplished what we set out to do.

Midcourse Corrections: We need to make midcourse corrections in our strategies when we discover they are not working, for God does not ask that we repeatedly butt our heads against brick walls. We keep correcting until we discover an approach that works. Our faith goals will be realized and we will experience the joy of victory in our lives.

As we persist, we can expect three results from implementing a faith plan. First, the goal will be reached, though it may not be in the way we expect or according to the timetable we envision. God does not mock or frustrate His children. If God gives us a vision of what He would like to see accomplished in an area of faith, and then confirms that vision in our hearts, we can be certain that He will also precede us with strategies that can make those visions realities. We probably will need to make midcourse corrections in our strategies, but, as God gives perseverance, we will eventually see the successful attainment of our goals. We need to be flexible in our timetables. We are not omniscient. Abraham learned the importance of adjusting his timetable to fit God's. Hang on to the goal, but expect adjustments with the dates.

God Will Be Glorified

A second result of implementing a faith plan is that *God is glorified*. When we accomplish the work we have been called to do on this earth, it is God who receives the glory (John 17:4).

In the example of Nehemiah, we learn that in spite of incredible opposition, he, and a remnant of Jews who had returned with him from captivity, rebuilt the wall in just 52 days (a modern-day engineering miracle)! Reflecting on the accomplishment, Nehemiah relates, "It came about when all our enemies heard of it, and all the nations surrounding us saw it, they lost their confidence; for they recognized this work had been accomplished with the help of our God" (Neh. 6:16).

When we realize a true faith goal, it will be obvious to those around us that our achievements have been made possible by God's direct intervention in our lives, and His name will be glorified.

Personal Growth

Third, we will experience *personal growth*. In the process of carrying out a faith plan, we have seen that faith-testing barriers inevitably arise. We read that we should actually welcome barriers, "consider[ing] it all joy ... when we encounter various trials," for the testing of our faith produces endurance in our character, and endurance leads to our ultimately becoming "perfect and complete."

The ball is now in *your* court! As you go about implementing your own faith plan, remember that you are involved in a unique partnership. God's part is to *direct* you in the way you should go, to *provide* for all your needs, and ultimately to *reward* you with success. We know that what "He [has] promised, He [is] able also to perform" (Rom. 4:21). Your part of the bargain is to have faith, which will sustain you throughout the entire faith-planning process and to act in accordance with that faith.

PERSONAL APPLICATION

Study the two examples on pages 93 and 94. You will notice that for each faith goal, a series of specific activities has been listed. Next to each activity is a projected start and finish date. On page 95 is a calendar for the six-month time period to use in implementing your faith goals. By using horizontal lines to represent the start and finish dates for the activities, you will have a visual monitor for both of your faith goals. Telling you what has to happen and by when. Note example on page 96.

Now turn to the worksheet on the next page and list the specific steps you need to take to implement your strategy. Then complete the top portion of the calendar on page 95, writing in the months and the beginning days of each week for the time period in which you will be working. Finally, using horizontal lines, graph the beginning and ending dates for each of your steps on the calendar.

Scheduling Activities
Worksheet

Faith Goal: _____

	ACTIVITIES	START	FINISH
1.	_____	_____	_____
2.	_____	_____	_____
3.	_____	_____	_____
4.	_____	_____	_____
5.	_____	_____	_____

Faith Goal: _____

	ACTIVITIES	START	FINISH
1.	_____	_____	_____
2.	_____	_____	_____
3.	_____	_____	_____
4.	_____	_____	_____
5.	_____	_____	_____

Scheduling Activities
Example 1

Faith Goal: Raise $200,000 in capital.

ACTIVITIES	START	FINISH
1. Develop a prospectus	Nov. 6	Dec. 4
2. Develop a list of potential investors	Dec. 4	Dec. 18
3. Send out prospectus	Jan. 1	Jan. 15
4. Make follow-up phone calls	Jan. 22	Feb. 12
5. Close out the partnership	Feb. 5	Mar. 18
6.		
7.		
8.		
9.		
10.		

Scheduling Activities
Example 2

Faith Goal:	Begin a neighborhood Bible study.		
ACTIVITIES		START	FINISH
1. Develop a core group to host the study		Oct. 9	Oct. 23
2. Send out invitations		Nov. 6	Nov. 20
3. Plan the outreach party		Nov. 20	Dec. 4
4. Conduct the party			Dec. 15
5. Begin the Bible study		Jan. 4	Mar. 4
6.			
7.			
8.			
9.			
10.			

Faith-Planning Chart
Worksheet

FAITH GOALS	ACTIVITIES	Week		Week		Week		Week		Week		Week	

Faith-Planning Chart
Example

FAITH GOALS	ACTIVITIES	OCT. Week				NOV. Week				DEC. Week				JAN. Week				FEB. Week				MAR. Week			
NEIGH-BORHOOD BIBLE STUDY	Develop a core group																								
	Send out invitations																								
	Plan party																								
	Conduct party																								
	Begin Bible study																								
RAISE $200,000 IN CAPITAL	Develop prospectus																								
	Develop list of potential investors																								
	Send out prospectus																								
	Follow-up phone calls																								
	Close partnership																								

9
Building Faith Muscle

In these last two chapters, I want to share how to apply faith-planning principles to our everyday walk with the Lord. In this chapter, we focus on how to build faith; in the last chapter, how to walk by faith.

What if a member of your immediate family suffered from a chronic illness that could only be cured by *your* faith? Such was the case of the man who brought his son to Jesus. He pleaded for Jesus to heal his son by saying, "But if You can do anything, take pity on us and help us!" (Mark 9:22)

Jesus responds, " 'If You can!' All things are possible to him who believes." In His reply, Jesus places the responsibility for the boy's healing on the faith of the father. It was at this point the father realized the weakness of his own faith and cried out, "I do believe; help me in *my* unbelief" (vv. 23–24).

Perhaps you have felt like the father at times. If you were really honest, you would have to admit, "I do believe, but help me in my unbelief." It could be that you have been a Christian for a number of years, but your faith has not grown with your age. Wherever you are in your Christian life, you need to build your faith. It is your faith that will allow God's resources to flow through you to areas of need that you contact each week. It is also your unbelief that restricts God's ability to work. "He [Jesus] could do no mighty work there because of their unbelief" (Matt. 13:58).

How do we build faith muscle? I suggest that building faith is a process requiring specific points of action on our parts. Just as we cannot turn from a 90-pound weakling to a he-man overnight, neither can we expect an instant cure for unbelief. Developing faith is an exciting adventure of spiritual growth.

I believe there are four action steps we can take to build and strengthen faith. I would like to illustrate these from the life of King Jehoshaphat. Jehoshaphat became king over Judah when he was 35 years old and ruled for 25 years. He was one of the few kings of Judah who walked with the Lord and did "right in the sight of the Lord" (2 Chron. 20:32). In one episode in the life of Jehoshaphat, we witness firsthand the four-step faith-building process in action.

Identify Our Need of the Lord

The sons of Moab had joined with the sons of Ammon and the Menunites to make war against Jehoshaphat. Their combined forces posed a formidable challenge to this righteous king of Judah. On hearing the news, King Jehoshaphat became fearful (2 Chron. 20:1–3). Even though he had a large army and had seen God work in past battles to provide victory, this new challenge produced fear.

Jehoshaphat was confronted with his faith challenge. A *faith challenge* is anything that comes into our lives that provides us opportunities to trust God specifically. In our goal-setting chapter, we called this a faith area. But here we are broadening the concept to include everything from threat of life to the day-to-day hassles of living.

Step one in building our faith, then, is to recognize that faith challenges that come our way are really opportunities for faith-building instead of calamities to be endured. Our perspectives will change as we understand three underlying truths: First, that trials give us opportunities for growth (James 1:1–3); that God will not allow anything to come into our lives that He has not first passed on and that He does not feel we are ready to handle with His help (1 Cor. 10:13); and that we are not to rely on feelings as the basis of our faith. Feelings are tied to circumstances. When Jehoshaphat learned of the size of the enemy army, he was frightened! Nothing wrong with that. When we are confronted with our faith challenges, we experience some fear and anxiety. It's part of our psychological makeup.

In summary, we need to develop a perspective of viewing the difficulties of life as a series of opportunities to trust God. Whether we are about to be invaded by an enemy army (as was the case of Jehoshaphat) or stranded with a flat tire en route to an important meeting—both are challenges to our faith and are opportunities to build stronger faith.

Focus on the Lord

"Jehoshaphat was afraid and turned his attention to seek the Lord" (2 Chron 20:3). Step 2 is to turn *from* what is causing fear and anxiety and turn *to* the Lord. Too often we become paralyzed by our problems and never shift our minds *to* the Lord. Unless we focus on the Lord we can never build our faith. It is the Lord who is the author and perfector of our faith (Heb. 12:2) and unless we focus on Him, we can only be defeated by our challenges.

Abraham struggled with faith-building after God had promised him that he would have children and become the father of many nations. Twenty-five years had passed and no children were in sight. Abraham contemplated the hopelessness of his situation by considering his own body, 100 years old, and that of his wife Sarah, 90 years old. But his focus did not remain on his hopeless situation. "Yet, with respect to the promise of God, he did not waver in unbelief, but *grew strong in faith,* giving glory to God" (Rom. 4:20). Abraham turned his attention 180 degrees from his bad situation to God. As a result, he "grew in his faith."

Sarah also was affected by this unique faith challenge. "By faith even Sarah herself received ability to conceive, even beyond the proper time of life, since she considered Him faithful who had promised" (Heb. 11:11).

Focusing on the Lord is to substitute thoughts of God for thoughts of the challenges we face. This is an act of our will in which we make choices of what will occupy our thoughts. We cannot simply say that we will not think of our hopeless situations, because to do so causes us to think of them. Instead, we make efforts to focus on the nature and character of God.

This is what Jehoshaphat did. "And he said, 'O Lord, the God of our fathers, art Thou not God in the heavens? And art Thou not ruler over all the kingdoms of the nations? Power and might are in Thy hand' " (2 Chron. 20:6).

One of the ways to focus on the Lord is to review the psalms that speak of God as a defender of those who trust in Him. As I do, my whole perspective changes. Instead of fear and anxiety, I experience a sense of excitement and anticipation of how my Father is going to meet my needs.

Some of the psalms passages I like to meditate on are:

I love Thee, O Lord, my strength.
The Lord is my rock and my fortress and my deliverer,
My God, my rock, in whom I take refuge;
My shield and the horn of my salvation,
my stronghold (18:1–2).

The Lord is my shepherd,
I shall not want (23:1).

The Lord is my light and my salvation;
Whom shall I fear?
The Lord is the defense of my life;
Whom shall I dread?
When evildoers came upon me to devour my flesh,
My adversaries and my enemies, they stumbled and fell.
Though a host encamp against me,
My heart will not fear;
Though war arise against me,
In spite of this I shall be confident (27:1–3).

Trust the Lord

In Step 3, we move from a general focus on God to a specific trust in Him to meet our faith challenge. We are to move from the position of "I believe God *can* do it" to "I believe God *will* do it."

Jehoshaphat shows us how to do this. He looked at how God had worked in the past in a similar situation. He reminded God and himself of how God drove out the inhabitants of the Promised Land to give it to the descendants of Abraham (2 Chron. 20:7). What an appropriate thought to dwell on! Jehoshaphat was being attacked by enemy forces, so what did he do? He reminded himself of how the Lord had wiped out other enemies in the past.

I believe one of the real problems in the Christian walk is the plague of "short memories." We forget too quickly the ways in which God has worked in the past to deliver us. We forget how He has met our needs when we were confronted with similar challenges. That is why the Lord commanded Joshua to build a monument of stones from the Jordan River to remind the people of His ability to meet their needs.

Perhaps every Christian family should keep a monument of

stones. Each stone could be labeled with a description of a specific time when God met a particular need. Wouldn't that make an interesting conversation piece when friends visit?

Jehoshaphat also reminded God of an earlier promise that "should evil come on us, the sword, or judgment, or pestilence, or famine, we will stand before this house and before Thee and cry to Thee in our distress, and Thou wilt hear and deliver us" (2 Chron. 20:9). To claim a promise from God is to *act* on it. All true faith requires an *action* step.

God's response was, "Do not fear . . . for the battle is not yours, but God's. Tomorrow go down against them. . . . You need not fight in this battle; station yourselves; stand and see the salvation of the Lord on your behalf. . . . Do not fear or be dismayed; tomorrow go out to face them, for the Lord is with you" (20:15–17).

God could have wiped out the enemy without Jehoshaphat and his troops preparing for battle, but I believe He was testing Jehoshaphat's faith by providing an action step. Again we see the two parts of a faith venture:

My part: To prepare for battle and station ourselves

God's part: To do the actual battle

Your challenge in Step 3 is first to know God's Word in such a way that you can identify and claim promises from it that relate to your faith challenge, and then to take your action step to move from intellectual assent to true faith.

Rest in the Lord

Jehoshaphat reminded himself and his people that they were powerless before such a great multitude, and he recognized that true faith was to depend on God coming through for them. The Lord responded to the king's faith by reassuring Jehoshaphat and the people that He was in charge.

This is the perspective we need to maintain. The battle is the Lord's: it is not our fight. "Cease striving and know that I am God" (Ps. 46:10).

PERSONAL APPLICATION

Identify your need *of* the Lord:

Identify a specific faith challenge that you face in your life.

_____

_____

_____

_____

Focus on the Lord. On what passages from God's Word can you meditate to shift your focus from the challenge and to God?

_____

_____

_____

_____

Trust in the Lord. Review how God has met your needs in the past.

_____

_____

Identify specific promises from Scripture that relate to your need.

_____

_____

_____

Rest in the Lord: Rest in the confidence that the battle is the Lord's; continue to meditate on God's attributes and His faithfulness.

10
Developing a Daily Faith Walk

Maintaining a consistent day-to-day walk with the Lord is one of the greatest challenges any of us will have. Often, it's easier to trust God when there's nowhere else to turn (as in the case of Jehoshaphat). Walking daily in fellowship with the Lord through the hurdles of mundane living—that's the challenge.

Enoch, another member of the Faith Hall of Fame, had a consistent daily walk with the Lord for 300 years. No battles, no crises. He walked *by faith* with the Lord. Faith-planning principles can help us develop more consistent walks with God.

Life's Greatest Goal
"What is your ultimate goal in life?" A college sophomore posed that question to me at a recent student retreat. He wanted to know which goals in my life I considered most important.

How would you answer that question? Would it be accomplishing great things, serving others, developing your potential to the fullest, meeting the needs of your family, leading others to Christ, discipling new believers, being successful in business, giving money to the Lord's work? What would you consider your ultimate life goal?

My four-year-old son, Brannon, is full of questions. He eagerly gains new knowledge, is energetic, and constantly on the go. If I ask Brannon what his ultimate goal in life is, he could only tell me his latest fad (last week he wanted to be a professional football player). If you asked me what *I* wanted for my son, I could give you a much better perspective by sharing with you the long-range goals I have in mind for his growth and development.

In the same way, we need to go to our heavenly Father to find out His perspective on developing our lives here on earth. Often in the hectic day-to-day struggle of living, we become caught up in fads. Some of these fads may be very well-intentioned, but they reflect our spiritual adolescence.

Our Father's ultimate goal for His children is "to become conformed to the image of His Son" (Rom. 8:29). We are to grow and develop in such a way that the qualities our Lord demonstrated on earth become our qualities. We are to live out His resurrected life. We are to experience daily the fruit of His Spirit—love, joy, peace, patience, kindness, gentleness and self-control (Gal. 5:22). We are to be progressing toward our ultimate goal which finally will be realized when we see Him face to face (1 John 3:2).

Unfortunately, too many Christians cannot identify with this lifestyle. Instead of progressing, we are regressing. Instead of growing toward God, we experience more of an up-and-down Christian walk—sometimes winning, but most often losing. We relate more to Paul's experience, "For the good that I wish, I do not do; but I practice the very evil that I do not wish" (Rom. 7:19).

One reason so many of us are not progressing toward our

ultimate life goal is that we have not discovered the reality that "The righteous man shall live by faith" (Rom. 1:17). Growth and victory occur as we learn to exercise faith on a consistent day-to-day basis. To conclude our study of faith planning, I want to share some thoughts on how to apply faith principles to the challenges we encounter in our spiritual pilgrimages of becoming more like Christ.

Is Christ in Your Life?

Several years ago, I was conducting a seminar in the Midwest. After I spoke on how we can know Christ personally, a young business executive approached me. I could tell that he was having a struggle with the basic concept that we can know God personally. I asked him, "Have you ever invited Jesus Christ to come into your life and to forgive your sins?" He replied, "I have been asking Christ to come into my life every day for the last two years!" "Where is He then?" I questioned. Hanging his head, he sighed, "I don't know."

What was his problem? He had not combined *faith* with his request for Christ to come into his life. In Ephesians we read, "For by grace you have been saved through faith; and that not of yourselves, it is the gift of God" (2:8).

We remember that faith has two parts—*My Part* (an area of action) and *God's Part* (an area of trust). As I considered with him various verses in the New Testament, it became clear to me that my friend believed he was separated from God and in need of a Saviour. He believed that Jesus had died on the cross to pay the penalty for his sin, but he still had not taken a step of faith. He had only intellectual belief. Turning to Revelation 3:20, I asked my friend to read aloud what Jesus promised. He read, "Behold, I stand at the door and knock; if anyone hears My voice and opens the door, I will come in to him, and will dine with him, and he with Me."

I asked him, "What does Jesus promise He will do (*God's*

Part)?" He reread the verse and then replied, "He says that He will come into my life." What is the *one* thing you must do according to this verse for Him to come into your life (*my part*)?" Looking at the verse again, he replied, "Open the door of my heart."

I suggested we bow in prayer and that he pray for the *last* time to invite Christ into his heart—by faith. After he prayed, he looked up with a smile. I asked him, "Where is Christ right now in relationship to you?" He hesitated only a moment and then replied, "He's in my heart." "How do you know?" "Because He said He would come in if I asked Him, and that's just what I did!"

My friend had discovered the reality of Christ coming into his life by faith. He had finally learned to simply believe that God would do what He had promised He would do.

In your life, perhaps you've walked down the church aisle to respond to an invitation or prayed a prayer, but have never really combined *faith* with your intellectual beliefs and, therefore, have never experienced the assurance that Christ is in your life. If not, I encourage you to ask Him into your life—by faith. It will be the *last* time, and you will find that "The Spirit Himself bears witness with our spirit that we are children of God" (Rom. 8:16).

Experiencing God's Forgiveness

Last fall I was traveling to Washington, D.C. via the "red-eye" special. (That's a plane that leaves late at night and arrives later still.) It was a cold, wet night, and after getting a cab at Washington's National Airport, I looked forward to a good night's rest before an early morning breakfast meeting. As we got closer to my motel, all I could see was a darkened building with candles flickering in the lobby. The motel had lost its power. An embarrassed desk clerk filled me in on what it would be like to stay in a motel with no power.

My room was on the 12th floor (long walk). Only emergency hall lights would provide lighting in my room, and I would have to leave my door open (dangerous in D.C. at night) to benefit from them. Along with that, there would be no water for showers in the morning.

Suddenly, it struck me. Here was a multimillion-dollar facility virtually worthless, because it had lost its power. Many of us as Christians lose our power source. We have God's Spirit living within us. We have access to His unlimited resources, but we allow unconfessed sins to build up in our lives and, as a result, we no longer experience His power in our lives.

David shared with us the effects of unconfessed sin in his life, "When I kept silent about my sin, my body wasted away. . . . Thy hand was heavy upon me; my vitality was drained away" (Ps. 32:3–4).

For every problem, God had made a provision. God's provision for sins that come into our lives is to confess them to Him. David continued, "I acknowledged my sin to Thee, and my iniquity I did not hide; I said, 'I will confess my transgressions to the Lord'; and Thou didst forgive the guilt of my sin" (Ps. 32:5).

We have a wonderful promise: "If we confess our sins, He is faithful and righteous to forgive us our sins and to cleanse us from all unrighteousness" (1 John 1:9). The word *confess* simply means to "agree with." Call sin—*sin!* Admit to God that you got angry, that you blew it at the office, and He will give you a spiritual bath.

What happens when we confess our sins to God and we don't feel forgiven? This was the plight of a friend of mine who was having a very difficult time experiencing God's cleansing and forgiveness in his life. Together we looked at 1 John 1:9 and I asked him, "What does God promise He will do (*God's part*)?" "Forgive and cleanse," was the reply. "Great," I exclaimed. "Now what is the *one* thing we have to do to experience His forgiveness and cleansing (*my part*)?" The light started to go on. He said, "It appears all I have to do is confess my sins to God."

"Only partially," was my reply. I went on to point out that he had to confess his sins *by faith,* believing that God would cleanse him, not because he said the words, but because he was putting his faith in God's promise to cleanse him.

You and I can claim this same provision for dealing with sins in our lives, but we must claim the promise by faith. Only then can God's cleansing power be experienced.

Being Controlled by the Holy Spirit

Several years ago, our team conducted a series of leadership-training seminars in Africa. Our tour took us to the tip of Africa where the South Atlantic and the Indian Oceans come together. The currents are so treacherous that ocean going vessels are instructed to take on pilots to guide them as they approach land fall. The remains of sunken ships in the harbor attest to the folly of captains who tried to make it without the aid of the trained pilots.

God never intended for us to try to make it through the treacherous currents of life on our own. He gives us His Holy Spirit to serve as our Pilot and Guide. Yet many Christians never relinquish control of their "ship" to the new Pilot and, as a result, their lives end up in wrecked conditions that God never intended.

Jesus told His disciples shortly before His death that it was really to their advantage that He go away because the Helper (Holy Spirit) would come (John 16). He later warned them not to leave Jerusalem until the Holy Spirit came to give them the power they would need to witness for Him.

In Paul's letter to the church at Ephesus, he commanded Christians, "Do not get drunk with wine, . . . but be filled with the Spirit" (5:18). Being filled with the Spirit is not an optional part of the Christian life. The Holy Spirit is to be our source of power and our Pilot to guide us that we might become all God intended. Being filled with the Spirit is to be controlled and empowered by God.

One summer my wife and I decided to take a raft trip down a portion of the Colorado River. As we drove beside the river to our staging area, I noticed the river was larger than the brochure had indicated. There also seemed to be more jagged rocks, and the current was much swifter. I thought, "I sure hope the raft is sturdy."

After arriving at the staging area, our group was divided into "raft teams" with six people in each group. Then they gave us a gas cylinder with instructions to hook up the valves in such a way that the gas could flow from the cylinder to the package. To my amazement, as the gas filled the package, it started to take the shape of a raft. It looked so much like a raft we decided to try it out on the river. To everyone's relief, it held us up all the way down our portion of the river. What had happened? Filling the package with the gas transformed it so that it possessed a structure and strength it normally didn't have.

Being filled with God's Spirit is to be controlled by the Holy Spirit in such a way that God's qualities actually are reflected through our personalities. When we're not normally loving, He can love through us. When patience is lacking, He can produce it in our lives.

We are to be God's "rafts." As we allow His Spirit to fill and control every area of our lives, our lives take on new shape and structure. Then, in the currents of life, we suddenly find ourselves able to withstand the jagged boulders that would normally sink us.

We are filled with the Spirit by faith. I have met Christians who sincerely desire for God's Spirit to control and fill them, but desire without faith produces only frustration. I have met other Christians who equate the filling of God's Spirit with feelings, but feelings come and go.

My part of being filled with the Holy Spirit is to *ask*. God's part is to fill me. I know He will because it's His will (Eph. 5:18). And I know too that if I "*ask* anything according to His will, He hears" (1 John 5:14). Being filled with God's Spirit is to be an everyday experience for the believer. We are to depend on God's resources to meet our needs.

How are we filled with the Holy Spirit? I believe the Bible teaches two essential steps. The first step is heart preparation. God will not fill a person who is not open to His lordship and control of all areas of life.

During a three-week stay in Africa, we spent one afternoon in a game park near Nairobi. There we heard how monkeys are captured for zoos in the United States. A shining metallic object is placed in a long-necked jar tied to a tree. As monkeys swing through the trees, their eyes catch the reflection of the sun on the shining object. Reaching into the jar poses no problem to them, but when they try to bring their closed fists through the narrow openings, they can't make it. To gain freedom, all the monkeys need to do is to let go of the worthless object. Instead, the monkeys sit by the jar holding onto the object until their captors come to take them away.

Sometimes we exchange spiritual freedom for some worthless (from the eternal perspective) desire, ambition, or thing. For one reason or another we are not willing to give over every area of life to the lordship of Christ. We must present every area of our lives to Christ (Rom. 12:1–2).

Confession is another part of heart preparation. God cannot fill a dirty vessel. Confessing all known sins to God must precede seeking His filling. We need to ask God to show us any area of our lives that is not pleasing to Him and confess those sins, claiming His forgiveness by faith.

The second step of being filled with the Holy Spirit is to be filled by *faith*. Desire and cleansing is not enough. We must claim God's promise (*His part*) by faith and act on it (*our part*). Asking by faith means that we believe God will do what He said He would.

Feelings come and go. Our confidence is in the certainty of God and His Word. If you have never experienced the filling of God's Spirit and His control in your life, present yourself by faith to God and ask for the filling of His Spirit by faith.

Growing by Faith

The story is told of a young man from the South who visited a friend in Wyoming in the middle of winter. One afternoon when the temperature was five degrees above zero, the two took a drive in the country. Seeing a frozen lake, they parked the car and decided to explore. The Wyoming native immediately headed toward the center of the frozen lake. The man from the South adopted a conservative strategy. He decided to explore around the edge of the lake, never venturing more than six feet from shore. To be extra cautious he even walked on tiptoes. Suddenly, he heard a loud roar. Turning his head, he saw a local farmer driving a huge tractor across the middle of the ice. He looked down at himself standing on tiptoes. What a contrast! The farmer on a tractor—he on tiptoes. What was the difference? The local farmer knew the ice; the visitor from the South did not.

A lot of Christians are fearfully tiptoeing around the edge of their relationship with God simply because they don't know how trustworthy He is. We must have a regular time alone with God daily—exploring His Word, talking to Him about the day, listening to His counsel, and developing a firsthand knowledge of Him.

I literally fight to preserve my 30 minutes quiet time with the Lord each morning. I have found that this daily time is absolutely essential to my spiritual walk. No matter how challenging the day, my faith muscle grows as I spend time with God in the Word. I venture forth with a confident assurance of God's absolute faithfulness.

If you do not have a regular time with the Lord each day, I encourage you to begin. Set aside a time and place that will minimize interruptions and develop a firsthand knowledge of your Father who loves you.

Are You Willing to Trust God?

God will not turn His back on a person who trusts Him with a clean heart and pure motives. Step out by faith. The purpose of this book is to help you learn to trust God more, to expose you to the power available when you are willing to trust God. Begin the exciting adventure of not only planning by faith— but living by faith.

‘PERSONAL APPLICATION

On the following pages is the Spiritual Survey we use in our seminars to help each of us identify the next step in our spiritual pilgrimage of becoming more like Christ. On each page, simply respond to the questions or directions.

One page deals with the assurance of salvation. On another you are asked to actually write out on a sheet of paper specific sins that God's Spirit brings to your mind. Right now, confess them to the Lord, then tear up the paper and throw it away to symbolize what God does when we confess our sins to Him. He removes them as far as the East is from the West. You also have an opportunity to respond to questions on God's filling you with His Spirit, and to identify steps you need to take in growing in your knowledge of God.

Spiritual Survey
Worksheet

ACCEPTANCE OF JESUS CHRIST AS SAVIOUR AND LORD BY FAITH

His Promise

"But as many as received Him, to them He gave the right to become children of God, even to those who believe in His name" (John 1:12).

"Behold, I stand at the door and knock; if anyone hears My voice and opens the door, I will come in to him, and will dine with him, and he with Me" (Rev. 3:20).

"For He Himself has said, 'I will never desert you, nor will I ever forsake you'" (Heb. 13:5).

My Response

Have I ever asked Jesus Christ into my life?   _____

Will Christ come into my life if I ask Him?   _____

Prayer: "Lord Jesus, I need You. Thank You for dying on the cross for my sins. I open the door of my life and receive You as my Saviour and Lord. Thank You for forgiving my sins and giving me eternal life. Take control of my life. Make me the kind of person You want me to be."

Did He come in as He promised?   _____

Will He ever leave me?   _____

CONFESSION OF SINS

His Promise

"If we confess our sins, He is faithful and righteous to forgive us our sins and to cleanse us from all unrighteousness" (1 John 1:9).

"And their sins and their lawless deeds I will remember no more" (Heb. 10:17).

My Response

On a separate sheet of paper make a list of the specific sins that the Holy Spirit reveals to you. Then confess them and claim God's promise of forgiveness in 1 John 1:9. Write 1 John 1:9 across the page, tear it up and throw it away to symbolize the fact that God forgives us and remembers our sins no more.

CONTROL: BEING FILLED WITH THE SPIRIT

His Promise

"And do not get drunk with wine, for that is dissipation, but be filled with the Spirit" (Eph. 5:18).

"And this is the confidence which we have before Him, that, if we ask anything according to His will, He hears us. And if we know that He hears us in whatever we ask, we know that we have the requests which we have asked from Him" (1 John 5:14-15).

"Blessed are those who hunger and thirst for righteousness, for they shall be satisfied" (Matt. 5:6).

"I urge you therefore, brethren, by the mercies of God, to present your bodies a living and holy sacrifice, acceptable to God, which is your spiritual service of worship" (Rom. 12:1).

My Response

Do I desire to be controlled by the Holy Spirit? _____

Have I presented every area of my life to Christ? _____

Will God fill me with His Spirit if I ask? _____

Prayer: "Dear Father, I need You. I have been in control of my life; and, as a result, I have sinned against You. I thank You that You have forgiven my sins through Christ's death on the cross for me. I invite Christ to again take control of my life. Fill me with the Holy Spirit as You *commanded,* and as You *promised* in Your Word if I ask in faith. I pray this in the name of Jesus. As an expression of my faith, I now thank You for taking control of my life and for filling me with the Holy Spirit."

Am I filled with the Holy Spirit? _____

How do I know? _____

STEPS FOR SPIRITUAL GROWTH

If you must answer No to any of the following questions, challenge yourself by filling in an Action Step:

Do I realize my purpose in life is to bring glory to God and become conformed to His image?

Yes ___ No ___ Action Step _____

116

Do I have a regular time each day when I can be alone with God?

Yes ___ No ___ Action Step _____

_____

Do I have a regular time for study of God's Word?

Yes ___ No ___ Action Step _____

_____

Do I know how to share my faith with others?

Yes ___ No ___ Action Step _____

_____

Do I now have particular opportunities in which I can trust God and build my faith?

Yes ___ No ___ Action Step _____

_____

Am I actively involved in a local church where I can grow and have fellowship with others?

Yes ___ No ___ Action Step _____

_____